EVERYDAY GAMES FOR SENSORY PROCESSING DISORDER

Everyday Games

— for —
Sensory Processing Disorder

100 Playful Activities
To Empower Children with
Sensory Differences

Barbara Sher, OTR

ALTHEA
PRESS

Contents

Foreword

Many years ago, as a new Occupational Therapist, I happened upon a book by another OT, Barbara Sher. It was packed with wonderful ideas and great activities to support children's development; it became one of my go-to guides as I started my own work. Since then, I have added many of Barbara's books to my library and have learned so much from every one. The one you're holding is the best one yet!

In today's world, many of us experience fractured attention that is constantly interrupted by media, current events, and the demands of daily life. However, Barbara has given us a choice in *Everyday Games*: to be conscious and carve out time to engage with our children and spend our precious attention on them. Within are the necessary tools to guide a child's development through engagement and mindfulness.

Children with SPD can have a range of needs. To that end, *Everyday Games* offers activities for touch, sight, balance, taste, smell, movement, sound, gross motor, and fine motor. Barbara's games speak to the need to be included and be a part of a group—which she details in a chapter on building social skills. Each chapter begins with a series of goals to help you understand the purpose of the games within the chapter, and how the skills build on one another. Although each activity can be tailored to suit a range of ages, modifications for older kids are included in some cases to encourage flexibility and accommodate your child's particular developmental abilities. All of these games are easy and inexpensive to implement with items found around the home. If the background information on SPD, and the 100 games weren't enough, Barbara has also included resources toys, a heavy work list for indoor and outdoor activities, and a collection of success stories illustrating the many ways play can lead to significant breakthroughs.

Throughout her career, Barbara has maintained that "attention is the elixir of brain development," and attention is most easily accessed when kids are playing and having fun. In *Everyday Games*, Barbara offers a positive, solutions-based approach with an emphasis on fun. Having fun together is empowering to children and parents—really, anyone who supports children's development, like therapists, teachers, camp counselors, and more, can all be inspired by the abundance of activities offered in this book.

Playfulness, fun, engagement and shared experiences build relationships that form the foundation of us all. Thank you, Barbara, for continuing to provide these wonderful activities and, reminding us about what is important for our children.

Enjoy reading, and let the fun begin!

Paula Aquilla, B.Sc., OT, Ontario, Canada

The Importance of Attention

I graduated from the first occupational therapy master's program at the University of Southern California, but I can't credit my classroom experience there for revealing to me the most important concept when working with children's development. It's this: Development is sequential. Each skill is built on the one learned before—it's a more exact and exquisite concept than "crawling comes before walking." It relates to all the learning domains, from motor skills to language development, intelligence, and social skills. They each set the foundation for lessons to come, though there are exceptions to the rule, and some children may skip stages, or learn lessons in other ways. However, here are some general examples:

- Most children need to accomplish seven distinct motor skills to grow from haphazardly swatting or grasping at an object to being able to hold a pencil correctly.

- Socially, children need to play beside others ("parallel play") before they can interact and play together.
- As most parents know, children learn how to take their clothes off before they are able to dress themselves independently.

It's my job to determine which stage a child is at developmentally, sort out where they might be stuck, and provide them with the learning experiences they need to grow to the next level. I've found the most effective way of doing this is in the form of games that open the door to therapy, as therapy is only effective when the child is engaged, and children are best engaged when they're having fun. A simple but crucial truth is that brain development depends on attention—attention is the elixir of brain development, and kids naturally pay attention when they are having fun. It's really as simple and important as that: Capture their attention. Development and elasticity of the brain happens with attention.

Paying attention is noticing what you are doing while you are doing it. It's being mindful of each moment exactly when it happens. When we are having fun and are engaged, we are attentive. All the games in this book are geared toward being interesting and novel and fun enough to warrant a child's attention.

Attention is essential, but there's another element: Children need to feel accepted just as they are, in the present moment. As a college student majoring in psychology at Boston University, I was very interested in how thoughts affect behavior. In my 45 years of practice since, I have seen how important it is for children, particularly those who have differences, to feel included, and I respect that need in the classroom. In an inclusive classroom, I may be introducing a game to target a special skill, such as balance, for one child with special needs, but I play the game with all the kids. This approach is two-pronged: I know all the kids in the class like to play and can always use some extra practice with balance, but on another, more important, level I do it so that the special-needs child will feel like part of the gang. I may provide a little extra help or modify the game when it's their turn to participate, but they still get to play along with everyone.

When I'm working one-on-one with a child and parent, I practice in much the same way, to respond to the child's desire to be accepted by helping that child feel successful. I'll begin with fun activities a young child can be successful at, before introducing games that present more of a challenge. I don't bring any fancy equipment or expensive toys; instead I show the family how they can help their child by using things found around the house or that can be purchased cheaply.

I have engaged children all over the world in play: from orphanages in Nicaragua; pediatric hospitals for cerebral palsy in Vietnam; a school for the deaf in Laos; therapy centers in Cambodia; preschools in remote Pacific islands; with Native American tribes in the south-western United States; at symposiums for professionals in Minnesota; at workshops in cosmopolitan cities such as San Diego, Vancouver, and Charlotte; and at universities in Hong Kong and all up and down the islands of New Zealand, to name a few. Each time, the children, teachers, therapists, and parents eagerly played the games and shared laughter and fun, because the concept of play crosses cultures and ages. Even in this age of electronic overload, these simple yet profound games are wanted and needed.

In my daily work, children happily greet me at the door with hugs. They know we will play a game, and kids love to play. Children on the sensory spectrum are not exceptions to the rule. They want to be engaged, and they want to be accepted—it doesn't matter if some wires in their nervous system are configured differently. The cause of a child's sensory dysfunctions doesn't matter quite as much as the solution, which is why I'm sharing these games with you. You can use these games at home in two ways: first, to reinforce and enhance your child's sensory system, and second—and more importantly and significantly—to take the time to play with your child.

Barbara Sher, OTR,
Saipan, Micronesia

It's a Busy World

Every day, we're bombarded with images and advertisements—even the volume on certain commercials is louder than most TV programs. In many schools, children, who developmentally learn through movement, are required to sit still for longer periods than ever before; physical education and recess time are severely shortened, and the respite of music and art classes has been cut back in many communities. This is the world our children are being born into. Is it any surprise that it feels like too much?

It is too much for many of us. Consider this: When was the last time you were free of distractions? Luckily, we as adults have learned our individual methods of coping. If we feel irritated by the television, we can turn it off and go read a book. If we have to sit in an office all day, we can go to the gym after work or work off stress in our own ways. We learn to ignore the loud construction crew working on the street where we are walking.

Children who feel their senses differently, either too strongly or not strongly enough, have to cope, too, but they don't always do it skillfully—they are kids, after all. When made to go into a crowded restaurant, a child who is over-responsive to sounds may have a meltdown—it's too much noise for that particular child to handle. When forced to sit still in a classroom, children who are under-responsive to their sense of balance may fall off a chair or stumble awkwardly during recess games. For any child, doing something about it (like getting up and leaving the noisy restaurant), is out of their control. So how can we blame them for their frustration?

Paradoxically, children with SPD can be over-responsive to one sense and under-responsive to another. And the same child can feel differently at different times. Sometimes what didn't bother them yesterday is clearly upsetting them today. And sometimes their reaction to a sensation will be appropriate, sometimes wildly unpredictable. It can be confusing and distressing for a parent, who may not even understand what the problem is.

A SOLUTION-BASED APPROACH

Since children respond in various ways on different days, we realize that the main way we can help our child is to make them more, not less, aware of their senses. When children are aware of their sensory systems and the information they're receiving, they—and we—can learn strategies for responding more appropriately.

For example, the child who won't touch anything messy with their hands can learn to manage their sensory reactions. We can help them work on building tolerance. We can guide them to notice when their tactile system is uncomfortable, and provide tools for an outlet to help control reactions. For instance, if a child with SPD is working with a project that involves glue, place a bowl of water nearby so hands can be washed whenever needed.

A child who is uncomfortable with the noise level in the grocery store can carry a portable music device loaded with calming sounds and favorite tunes in case the noise level gets uncomfortably high. The child who needs a certain amount of movement can try (with the help of a teacher or parent) sitting on a gym ball or slightly deflated beach ball to incorporate the necessary stimulation. This child may thrive with the responsibility of heavy work, like carrying groceries from the car.

Children on the sensory spectrum can learn, with our help, how to cope when one of their senses feels assaulted. We can help them identify the issue. Depending on their age, we can talk with them about it. Then we can help them figure out what to do about it.

When we thoughtfully guide them with playful sensory experiences, we help promote children's ability to process and integrate sensory information so they can respond in a positive way to their environment.

EXPLORING THE GIFT OF SENSES

There is a great advantage in helping children become more aware of sensory information: Homing in on one sense can be an exquisite experience for everyone involved. The timeless pleasure that comes from tasting an orange slice with our eyes closed is sublime. Smells, like the smell after a rain or the scent of a rose, can be transporting.

And the reactions to smelling cinnamon, peppermint, or other scents is strong and effective enough that an entire therapy—aromatherapy—was created around it. The velvety-soft fur of a cat or the feel of a cashmere sweater can delight your fingertips. And you don't have to convince a lover of classical music the heights one can reach by listening to a Mozart concerto with your whole sense of hearing.

Our job, and the intent of the games in this book, is to increase awareness of the child's sensory system, whether it's too high or too low. It's all about drawing in their attention and learning to pay attention ourselves. Attention is how brains develop and how sensory systems can mature. Once the awareness is there, children can learn, with our help, what is needed to make their life sweeter. And we, the adults tasked with helping, will benefit from the process, because we will delight in sharing experiences and seeing the world through the uncomplicated lens of a child.

Part

1

Digging in to Sensory Processing Disorder

Our senses play a major role in dictating our reaction to the world. We have many senses, and we may be more or less sensitive to certain stimuli in the world around us depending on our genetic makeup or even the time of day. Our sense of taste might be heightened when we are hungry, or conversely, desensitized when we're full. The sense of smell might be extremely acute during pregnancy. Our sense of hearing might be on full alert when we're lying in bed with the lights out.

But for children with Sensory Processing Disorder (SPD), their increased or diminished sensitivity to specific stimuli is always extreme—and it can affect life in a variety of ways.

SPD in Brief

We all have sensory preferences. Our noses look forward to the smell of coffee brewing in the morning. We stay a little longer in the shower because the feel of water pressure on our back is so pleasant. For some, a crooked hanging picture looks irritatingly wrong, and others would never ever go on a roller coaster.

A child with SPD finds it difficult to process and act upon certain information received through the senses. Typically, our nervous system receives messages from the senses, such as the sounds we hear and the food we taste, and we turn them into appropriate motor and behavioral responses. If a sound is too loud, we cover our ears. If a food tastes bad, we spit it out.

SPD is characterized by either a hypersensitivity (over-responsiveness) or hyposensitivity (under-responsiveness) to one's surroundings due to the brain's inability to properly integrate multisensory input. While all children may be quirky or particular about their likes and dislikes, children with SPD can be so affected by their sensory preferences that it interferes with normal everyday functioning. Children with hypersensitivity to sensory input may exhibit fearful responses to touch, textures, noise, crowds, lights, and smells, even when these inputs seem benign to others.

The sensory signals of a child with SPD may have difficulty organizing into an appropriate response. A child with SPD may "need" to touch everything and be overly affectionate, not understanding the idea of personal space. They may seek out things that vibrate, such as the washing machine, dishwasher, motorized toothbrush, or toys. They may lick, mouth, or chew non-food objects, or constantly smell objects. They may prefer strong foods such as lemons, hot sauce, and pickles, and/or strongly textured foods.

FOUR STAGES OF PROCESSING SENSATIONS

Everyone processes the sensations around them. And everyone's body does it differently. But all people, with or without SPD, unconsciously go through these four stages when encountering sensory input:

1. **REGISTRATION.** We become aware of a sensation physically. (Sound waves, for example, change the air pressure.)

2. **ORIENTATION.** We pay attention to the sensation. (For example: "That's a familiar sound.")

3. **INTERPRETATION.** We bring in prior information, memories, and knowledge already stored in our brains.

We then like the sensation, don't like it, or feel neutral about it. (The sound is an ice cream truck.)

4. **ORGANIZATION.** We use information to elicit a response: We avoid, ignore, or seek more. ("Mommy, where's the ice cream truck? I want to see it.")

If there is a dysfunction in the perception and the interpretation of the sense, there will be a problem in the response. Perhaps, in the example of a fire siren, a child with hypersensitivity to sound will cover their ears or cry.

THE SPD RESPONSE TO SENSORY INPUT

The average person will simply process sensory information without thinking much about it. But children with SPD respond to sensory input in one of three less-than-typical ways:

1. They under-respond to sensory input.
2. They over-respond to sensory input.
3. They seek/crave sensory input.

When a sensory system is under-responsive, it does not notice or respond to certain stimuli the way a typical sensory system would. Consider a child who doesn't notice when she is hurt, doesn't realize where a particular sound is coming from, or only wants crunchy food.

Children who are over-responsive to sensory input are more sensitive to sensory stimulation than most people. Their bodies feel sensation too easily or too intensely. They may try to avoid or minimize sensations or show inappropriate reactions to certain stimuli by being fearful or bothered. Perhaps you've noticed your child withdraws from being touched, covers their ears to avoid loud sounds, or avoids playground equipment because it's too scary.

When a sensory system craves sensory input, it drives the child to actively seek out certain sensory stimulation to feel satisfied. A child who craves tactile input may have to touch everyone, even if we see it as socially inappropriate. The child who wants more information from their nose may smell everything. Some visual children are irresistibly drawn to bright or moving objects, and a child craving more movement will be hyperactive and restless.

History and Misdiagnosis

Pioneering occupational therapist and neuroscientist A. Jean Ayres, PhD, likened SPD to a neurological "traffic jam" that prevents certain parts of the brain from receiving the information needed to interpret sensory information correctly. She feels the systems most often affected are the ones for movement, touch, and balance (proprioceptive, tactile, and vestibular).

Lucy Jane Miller, PhD, OTR, another pioneer and the author of *Sensational Kids: Hope and Help for Children with Sensory Processing Disorder (SPD)*, explained how children could be misdiagnosed, as many health-care professionals are not trained to recognize sensory issues. She says, "In children whose sensory processing of messages from the muscles and joints is impaired, posture and motor skills can be affected. These are the 'floppy babies' who worry new parents, and the kids who get called 'klutz' and 'spaz' on the playground. Still other children exhibit an appetite for sensation that is in perpetual overdrive. These kids often are misdiagnosed and inappropriately medicated for ADHD."

Discussions about a child's diagnosis can be confusing and even stressful. What parents should remember is that each child is unique—as we well know—and the approach used depends on what the individual child needs, not on their diagnosis.

THE SENSORY SPECTRUM

Like most disorders, symptoms of SPD occur within a broad spectrum of severity. A 2009 study by the Child Mind Institute found that one in every six children has sensory issues that make it hard to learn and function in school. Further, they add that while sensory processing issues are often seen in autistic children, they can also be found in those with Attention Deficit Hyperactivity Disorder (ADHD), Obsessive-Compulsive Disorder (OCD), and other developmental delays—or with no other diagnosis at all. Children may have differences to varying degrees in the way they process sensory information, or they may have anywhere from minor to severe difficulties, but overall, SPD is considered a disorder in which everyday life is disrupted.

One problem can lead to others. SPD kids might have problems with motor skills and other abilities needed for school success. As a result, they may become socially isolated and lose the ability to make friends or be a part of a group. They might have poor self-esteem, struggle academically, and be labeled as clumsy, unco-operative, or disruptive if the disorder is not treated effectively.

TREATMENT

SPD children are as intelligent as their peers and often are intel-lectually gifted; for example, they may learn to read earlier than others. However, because their brains may be wired differently, they need activities and strategies that suit their need to either increase their awareness of their senses or decrease their sensitivity. As a general rule, a child whose nervous system is on "high trigger / too wired" needs more calming input, while the child who is more "sluggish / too tired" needs more arousing input.

Your first course of action may be occupational therapy with a sensory integration, which incorporates a whole-body approach by providing playful activities and games. Games foster appropriate responses to sensation in an active, meaningful, and fun way, and over time the child is able to learn to better read their senses. As they build on their ability to tune out or respond effectively to

Are SPD and Autism the Same?

SPD kids are sometimes misdiagnosed with autism or placed on the autism spectrum. However, there are marked differences. Autism is usually characterized by impairments in communication and social interaction, and by repetitive behaviors (such as self-stimulation, or "stimming"). Sensory issues may play a large role in any of these factors, but someone with Autism Spectrum Disorder (ASD) usually experiences other symptoms besides sensory issues.

According to the Sensory Processing Disorders Organization, high rates of SPD are often found in children with autism, as these two conditions do coexist but are separate. The child with social and communication skills and no repetitive behaviors may very well have SPD and not autism.

distracting sights, sounds, and touches or to tolerate more sensations, this will help them focus, learn, and fit in at school.

Other effective methods include brain-training techniques and
concentrated work on specific motor and cognitive skills.

In all methods, parents are encouraged to get involved and to
learn, along with their child, which strategies and activities work
best for their sensational child at home. The bottom line for any
therapy at home, school, or the clinic is the joyful engagement of
the child. If it's fun for them, they will pay attention and learn.

The 10 Most Common Sensory Issues in Children with SPD

Every child is unique, just like every human is one of a kind. And yet humans share certain characteristics that are common. Many of us know the feelings of envy, doubt, sadness, joy, and sorrow, among others. Children with sensory-processing issues also have some characteristics in common, which is why the games and ideas in this book are geared to these issues.

1. WON'T TOUCH MESSY THINGS (TACTILE)

Most children have some opinion about the kinds of things they like—and don't like—to touch. Fuzzy kittens and warm bubbles are nearly universal in their appeal to children, while fewer young children like sticking their hand inside a pumpkin to pull out the slimy guts and seeds—and very few care to touch a thorn on a rose bush! But for children with SPD, this goes much deeper than just a preference. It's a preoccupation, even a compulsion, to want to feel or not feel certain things.

A child who is hyper-responsive (over-responsive) to touch may

- avoid or be bothered by light touch;
- be bothered by certain fabrics, textures or clothes;
- be bothered by tags on clothing;
- avoid or be bothered by messy substances on hands or face;
- have an aversion to normal skin-contact interactions (cuddling, hugs, kisses, and, sadly, even wiping after the restroom);
- get very upset by minor cuts or bug bites;
- desire deep pressure;
- squeeze themselves into tight places;
- lie underneath mattresses; or
- prefer heavy blankets.

A child who is hypo-responsive (under-responsive) to touch may

- touch people (yes, even when it's inappropriate);
- have an innate desire to touch all textures;
- desire rough play or messy activities;
- seek out tight places (same as hypersensitive);

- like lying underneath mattresses (same as hypersensitive);

- prefer heavy blankets (same as hypersensitive); or

- possess an unusually high or low pain threshold.

2. GETS DISTRACTED EASILY (VISUAL)

Children tend to notice things that adults overlook. That is one of the beautiful things about childhood. But children with SPD may be more—or less—impacted by all the bright, shiny, whirling things in the world around them.

Children who are hyper-responsive (over-responsive) to visual stimulation may:

- be bothered by bright or fluorescent lights;

- be bothered by patterns;

- have trouble reading high-contrast materials (such as black on white); or

- squint, blink, or rub their eyes frequently.

Children who are hypo-responsive (under-responsive) to visual stimulation may:

- seek out visual stimulation;

- have a great attraction to light;

- stare at objects, particularly moving ones; or

- demonstrate fascination with mirrors and shiny objects.

3. HAS TROUBLE WITH BALANCE (VESTIBULAR)

All children must learn to balance. For some it takes a little time. Others seem to be born with an innate ability to climb, teeter, and balance. Below are some signals of SPD related to balance. Children who are hyper-responsive (over-responsive) to their sense of balance may

- be fearful of falling;
- have gravitational insecurity;
- not like their feet to leave the ground; or
- have poor balance, perhaps falling often.

Children who are hypo-responsive (under-responsive) to their sense of balance may

- not notice if they fall;
- not be able to regain balance;
- fall easily; or
- spin without getting dizzy.

4. FUSSY ABOUT FOOD / PICKY EATER (GUSTATORY)

It's no coincidence that children's menus all include chicken tenders, grilled cheese, and hot dogs; most kids like them. But for children who have gustatory-related SPD, the underlying issues relate to heightened or decreased sensitivity to the tastes and textures that enter the mouth.

Children who are hyper-responsive (over-responsive) to oral stimulation may:

- be sensitive to food textures;
- be sensitive to having their teeth brushed;
- be a very picky eater (for example, only likes custard);
- encounter oral-motor and feeding problems;
- have speech/language delays; or
- prefer to eat the same things every day.

Children who are hypo-responsive (under-responsive) to oral stimulation may:

- seek out oral stimulation;
- seek out strong-tasting foods (such as spicy foods, lemons, pickles, and hot sauce);
- chew and suck on things (such as pencils, shirtsleeves, the neck of the T-shirt, or other objects); or
- prefer strong textures (ice cubes, crunchy foods, pretzels).

5. CAN'T STAND CERTAIN SMELLS (OLFACTORY)

Who likes the smell of gasoline being pumped at the gas station? The aroma of garlic and oil heating on the stovetop? We all have our favorites and not-so-favorites. But these simple sensations can affect the child with SPD tenfold, sometimes with troublesome consequences.

A child who is hyper-responsive (over-responsive) to smells may

- be distressed or nauseated by odors;
- notice odors others don't; or
- become agitated and have a meltdown or tantrum.

A child who is hypo-responsive (under-responsive) to smells may

- seek out the smell of everything around them; or
- seek out distasteful smells, like garbage and feces.

6. CAN'T SIT STILL / HYPERACTIVE / SEEKS SENSATION (PROPRIOCEPTIVE)

Almost every child likes movement. But when moving elicits fear or seems almost constant, SPD may be present. Children who are hyper-responsive (over-responsive) to movement may:

- demonstrate sensitivity to movement;
- avoid swings and fast-movement activities;
- become carsick easily;
- appear unreactive and slow;
- prefer sedentary activities over physical play; or
- rock to calm down.

Children who are hypo-responsive (under-responsive) to movement may

- engage in excessive movement, fidgeting, wiggling, spinning, jumping, and climbing;
- enjoy rough-and-tumble activities;
- seek fast-movement activities;
- be able to spin without getting dizzy;
- need to constantly fidget or move around; or
- have trouble sitting still.

7. HAS A SENSITIVITY TO SOUND (AUDITORY)

In this noisy world, where children don't necessarily have a say over their surroundings, children with SPD (and even those without!) can easily find themselves overwhelmed. It doesn't matter whether you're at a football game or sitting around the dinner table—any forum can impact a child with SPD.

Children who are hyper-responsive (over-responsive) to their sense of sound may

- be easily distracted by noise;
- make their own noise to drown out other sounds;
- dislike noisy appliances (vacuum cleaner, blender, dishwasher);
- put up a fight when entering noisy places;

- respond fearfully or strongly to sudden, high-pitched, loud, or metallic noises;

- notice background noises others don't seem to hear;

- frequently ask people to be quiet—to stop talking or singing; or

- run away, cry, or cover their ears when exposed to loud or unexpected sounds.

Children who are hypo-responsive (under-responsive) to their sense of sound may

- seek out noisy situations or specific noises;
- make noise to themselves or make noise "for noise's sake";
- not respond to verbal cues (even when called by name);
- like excessively loud music or television;
- seem oblivious to certain sounds;
- not be able to tell where sounds are coming from;
- not understand or remember things said to them (may need directions repeated);
- often ask, "What?";
- talk themselves through tasks; or
- not have been very vocal as infants.

8. IS UNCOORDINATED/CLUMSY (GROSS MOTOR)

Some children seem to be born athletes, while most others land in the middle of the competitive road. For children with gross motor SPD, however, physical victories are much harder earned. Children with SPD relating to gross motor skills may:

- find it difficult to plan movement;
- have poor motor coordination;
- move awkwardly or appear clumsy;

- be delayed in crawling, walking, running, climbing stairs, or catching a ball;

- have low or high muscle tone; or

- find it difficult to learn/follow exercise or dance steps.

9. HAS POOR HANDWRITING (FINE MOTOR)

 Nobody's born with fine motor skills—these take years to develop. However, children with fine motor SPD can benefit from extra help in the areas that require dexterity.

Children with SPD relating to fine motor skills may:

- have difficulty writing;
- have poor or illegible handwriting;
- break pencil points;
- find it difficult to button or snap fasteners, or string beads;
- drop things constantly;
- have difficulty dressing and eating;
- use inappropriate force to handle objects; or
- have delays in skills (such as coloring or cutting with scissors).

10. IS SOCIALLY UNCOMFORTABLE (SOCIAL)

Most everyone wants to be liked, have friends, and fit in, but social skills come more naturally to some than others. And while children with social-skills SPD might prefer to be left alone, the right coaching and guidance can help them learn the benefits of enjoying the company of others, making friends, and being a friend. Children with SPD related to social skills may:

- avoid crowds and noisy places;
- have difficulty making friends;
- be seen as a "loner";

- seem fearful of crowds or avoid standing in close proximity to others;
- be socially awkward; or
- be uncomfortable or get easily overstimulated in group settings.

Why Play at Home?

Play is crucial for young children. It helps them learn how to work their brains and move their bodies, expands their social skills, promotes problem solving and the ability to focus, and, best of all, helps them feel happy with themselves.

We're seeing now what happens when children don't have time to play. In the schools where recess is shortened, physical education—what we used to call "gym class"— is left out, and the emphasis is on sitting for long periods, children begin to have problems. They fidget; they don't pay attention; they have poor postural control and fall out of their chairs; anxieties rise and social skills deteriorate. When they aren't in school, many are sitting in front of screens, and in some communities it may not be safe to play outside. What can we do? Read on.

RADICALLY OLD-FASHIONED GAMES

What I'm advocating is radical in an old-fashioned way and can fit right into the home. Within this book, I've included games that will remind you of those from days gone by, that are still valid, useful, and fun. For example, a wonderfully simple way to help children learn balance is to bounce them on your lap—an activity that comes naturally to most parents with young children. Decorating cookies has a sweet reward, but it's also a fabulous way for your child to practice fine motor control. Timed races teach coordination and focus, egg hunts work on attention and vision, and so on.

Games are important learning strategies. You'll be reminded of childhood games in these sensory-rich activities, and you'll learn

new ones that are just the right fit for you and your child. Every activity is layered and combines a variety of modalities: movement, touching, vision, and interaction. Every dimension of sense is engaged—that's why these games are especially good for children with sensory differences, but they can be used to enhance the skills of all children.

Activities that perk up or calm down your child are not just effective in the moment; they actually help restructure the nervous system over time. Eventually, these children will be able to better tolerate challenging sensations and situations, regulate alertness, increase attention span, and limit sensory-seeking and sensory-avoiding behaviors. Just like you may doodle in a notebook to help stay awake at meetings or take a long walk to unwind, children need to engage in stabilizing, focusing activities, too.

PARENTS ARE THE BEST OBSERVERS

As a parent, your observation and awareness of your child's sensory reactions matter a lot. You've got a bird's-eye view into your child's most intimate moments. If you really look at what they are doing, they are telling you with their behaviors, what they need and prefer. What do they avoid? What do they want more of?

Your job may be to take what your child already does and redirect them to a safer, more effective way to get the same input. And, always, it needs to be fun! When you make the activity fun, you respect their need to be a kid, and you will together develop important skills that help them succeed—all while making wonderful memories that perhaps, one day, they will pass down to their own children.

14 Ways to Encourage Playfulness

1. **Make it a challenge.** "Can you jump over *both* cans?" or "I bet you can't hit that target!"

2. **Give them positive names.** "Okay, 'Mr. Sharp Eyes,' can you find Waldo?" or "Hey, 'Jumping Bug,' can you jump from here all the way to there?" or "Oh, 'Ms. Music Expert,' what's the name of this tune I'm humming?"

3. **Make inanimate things animate.** "Mr. Toaster is making a special piece of toast just for you," or "Can you jump over Ms. Cushion?"

4. **Have "Disney" days.** Have conversations with animals, bugs, plants, pets. Thank trees for shade, bowls for holding cereal, and so on.

5. **Add thinking skills.** "I gave you four crackers, and you ate one—how many do you have left?"

6. **Act exasperated or tell them what *not* to do.** "What, you *ate* one? I'm going to give you one more, but don't eat it!" or "Whatever you do, do *not* jump on my shadow!"

7. **Add the element of time with a stopwatch or second hand.** "Can you run around the tree and be back here in 12 seconds? Wow! Now, can you do it in 8 seconds?"

8. **Have "opposite day" any day.** "We're eating our decorated cookies before dinner 'cause it's opposite

continued ▶

continued ▶

day!" or "You have to go through the obstacle course backward because it's opposite day!"

9. **Do a "voice-over."** Pretend to be an announcer and describe what they are doing while they are doing it. If they are jumping on a trampoline, announcing their "feats" will inspire them to make some up.

10. **Use movement and song.** Whenever possible, add movement and song to your activity. Sing a song while tidying up, or do a silly dance washing dishes.

11. **Take turns.** It's fun if your child knows that their turn is next and you have to do what *they* say. Let them be the leader!

12. **Bring in nature.** Taking movement activities outdoors naturally adds more sensations. The smells, the feel of the air, the sense of space all add to the joy.

13. **Add water.** Being held by water in a pool or ocean is already a wonderful feeling, and it's perfect for the tactile- and movement-resistant child. It's easier to move and touch in a fluid environment.

14. **Include others.** If you can, bring in another child to demonstrate. Seeing an adult do things can be "so what" moment, but seeing another child do it . . . Now *that's* cool.

A TWOFOLD PAYOFF

This book focuses on solving problems, but it's about much more than that. Whether you have a regular time at home for playtime or fit in some spontaneous fun here and there, you will find that both you and your child thrive by playing games and by being totally present with each other. For that moment, e-mails and phone calls can wait. You'll know you are in the moment when you notice how absolutely beautiful your child is.

Children deeply appreciate a parent who will play with them, and parents deeply appreciate being loved by their child. There's no greater gift you can give or receive.

Part 2

Games & Activities

Now it's time to get down to business. The next 10 chapters each focus on a facet of SPD, detailing fun and simple games that are sure to capture children's attention—and strengthen the sensory areas they might need help in tempering.

In my professional work, I tend to focus on children up to five years of age—the years before brain cells start weeding themselves out and atrophying from disuse. For at-home use, and with a few exceptions, these games are best suited for children aged two, when children become able to follow directions, to kids aged twelve, when they may even start applying their own modifications.

These games are tried-and-true, but they are also guidelines—you will use many as they are, but I hope you will modify them to suit your child's needs and interests as you wish. Though I have been bringing therapeutic games to children for many years with great success, nobody knows your child or what she needs or enjoys like you do. Have fun!

Games for Touch

The sense of touch is usually associated with the feeling on the tips of our fingers, but in actuality the nerve endings that tell us about temperature, touch, pain, and pressure are all over our body. The tactile system is our largest sensory system.

Children on the sensory spectrum who are oversensitive to touch (hypersensitive or "tactile defensive") might be having a hard time because they are distracted by the irritating feeling of the labels inside the back of their T-shirt. Or they can't concentrate because they don't like the "itchy" feel of their polyester shirt. More typically, these are the children who get upset when their hands get dirty. They will absolutely not touch glue or any other sticky—and in their opinion, yucky—substance.

On the other hand, children who are undersensitive (hyposensitive) to their tactile information might not notice when their skin is scraped or they are touching something too hot. They might want to touch everything to get more stimulation, which clearly is not always appropriate or safe.

GOALS OF THE GAMES

The task at hand for children who are hypersensitive is to decrease their sensitivity and increase the number of textures they will tolerate. We might, at first, have to provide water nearby or gloves when they first experiment with a variety of textures, but little by little and substance by substance, we can help them tolerate the messier aspects of life or work around them.

For children who are hyposensitive, we want to increase their awareness of their skin by giving them a variety of experiences that help them notice differences.

And always, we want to engage their attention by making each activity interesting and fun for them.

Ice Cube Fun | 6 MONTHS TO 2 YEARS

It's time to make dinner, but your little one wants your attention. This is a good moment to introduce the novelty of fun with ice cubes. Grab for the slippery ice, chase it around a tray or surface, or suck on cold fingers—all great ways to get a child who tends to avoid messy things engaged in a tactile experience. It's not a new texture—it's just cold water!

Begin by putting just one cube in front of your child and watching their reaction. If it's positive, perhaps two ice cubes would be more fun? One cube can be flicked or slid to bang into another. Many cubes can be stacked on top of each other. Trying to stack slippery cubes is a fun challenge in itself! Also, depending on the child's age, keep an eye on the size of the melting cube so it's not small enough to swallow. Just replace the small one with another big cube.

If you plan ahead and add food coloring to the water before you freeze them into cubes, you'll increase the attraction. Who could resist a red ice cube and a blue ice cube swirling around in a soon-to-be purple puddle! (Yes, washing the coloring off their hands afterward might be another game!)

You could also use the ice cube game to increase tolerance for fruits or take advantage of certain preferences. Squish up fruits such as blackberries or raspberries, and freeze them for tastier fun!

Want to go beyond ice cubes for more novelty that will capture a child's interest? Try Jell-O squares, which are also fun to watch shimmy and shake—until your child pops them in their mouth, of course.

Mitten on a Bottle | 6 MONTHS TO 2 YEARS

When babies are old enough to hold their own bottle, even they can play a sock game that will enrich their sensory experience. You can do this the easy way by slipping a sock or mitten over a bottle. Use a variety of mittens or socks to get a variety of colors, textures, and patterns.

First, hold the covered bottle at eye level and talk about it as a way of introducing new concepts such as color and materials. "Here's a nice red wool sock for your bottle!" Your infant is just starting to integrate their senses, so this activity combines touch with sight.

On other days when you switch bottle covers, you can add the element of surprise and enhance your infant's ability to notice and feel differences. A baby who has enough safe and happy experiences with their senses is likely to decrease sensory issues early.

Water Play Games | 6 MONTHS TO 2 YEARS

Playing with a variety of objects in water is an excellent way to help a child who is extra-sensitive to touch. Water is a friendly medium and is not threatening to the tactile sense, so it's a safe place to experiment with textures.

You can introduce water play by filling up a large basin or bucket, putting the child in front of a sink, or letting your child sit in a tub full of water.

Gather materials such as the following ahead of time:

- sponge
- turkey baster
- eyedropper or medicine
- dropper

- funnel
- empty, clean spray bottle
- Ping-Pong balls

- ice cubes
- shaving cream corks
- straws

You can introduce the variety of materials one at a time or all at once. Doing them one at a time gives you an opportunity to play one-on-one with your child to demonstrate how to use the materials. For example, you can

- show your child how to soak up the water with a textured sponge and then squeeze it out;
- fill up a turkey baster, eyedropper, or medicine dropper with water and squirt it out;

- use a funnel to pour water into a cup (a plastic bottle cut in half can make a funnel and a cup—tape the edges if needed);

- use spray bottles to fill and aim at targets;

- catch floating Ping-Pong balls or ice cubes;

- put dabs of shaving cream in the water to push into a pile; or

- blow corks with a straw and watch them move about in the water.

Sometimes it's fun to introduce each experience one by one and talk about the feelings and actions. How about saying, "Let's push the squishy shaving cream dots together into one pile!"

Other times, you might just dump all the materials into the water in an open-ended kind of play and let your child experiment with them all, finding the ones that are personal favorites.

Where Am I Touching? | 1 YEAR TO 7 YEARS

In this touching game that requires no materials, ask your child to close their eyes and tell you where they are being touched. For example, put your finger on their knee or neck or elbow. Can he say where he is being touched? If he doesn't talk yet or know his body parts, can he then touch you in the same spot?

Use your finger to touch a body part, or add variations by using a feather or a cotton ball instead. Another possibility, which would further sensitize tactile awareness, is blowing on various parts of the body with a straw. Can your child feel where the blown air touches their body?

You can also strengthen a child's tolerance to different textures by changing the game and rubbing parts of his body with a variety of

materials instead. For example, rub your child's back with swatches of different textures, such as silk, velvet, wool, cotton, corduroy, or polyester. Talk about the differences with your darling: "Isn't this velvet soft? It's so soft. Feel this corduroy. It's a bit rougher, isn't it?" Ask your child to choose which one feels the best.

This aspect of the touching game will also give you information about the best kind of clothing textures to buy. It's nice to wear your favorite material.

Scarf Game | 1 YEAR TO 10 YEARS

Gather as many scarves as you can for this fun game. You could pick some up at a secondhand store or garage sale. Aim for a variety of textures—silk, chiffon, woven, wool, polyester, and so on. Your aim is to help your child strengthen her ability to touch different textures. Your mode is the fun of catching.

Start the game with the element of surprise to capture your child's attention. Walk into the room with a box full of scarves and casually dump the whole box—beautiful scarves fluttering here and there. Spend some time admiring the different varieties and colors.

Find all the red ones, for example, and count how many. Admire an especially pretty design. Ask your child to find their favorite.

From there, show your child how to play catch with a scarf. Playing catch with a scarf is so much simpler than with a ball. It works on the same eye-hand-coordination principle, but it's much easier to master.

Start by doing it together. You gently toss up a small scarf, then put your hands in just the right place so that you then have the ease of catching it as it comes softly fluttering down. Then, keep tossing your scarves higher and higher, with your hands anticipating where the scarf will land.

Another game is to snatch the scarf out of the air as it's falling down. Throw it up, watch it as it's floating down, and grab it! Do it with the right hand, then the left hand. See which one is better at catching.

Or change the game completely by encouraging your child to wrap themselves with all the scarves, which will increase their whole body's tolerance for touch.

MODIFICATIONS FOR OLDER KIDS To increase the challenge, play "catch the scarves" using two scarves! Try juggling with three. Or try playing catch with one heavy scarf and one light scarf—they fall at different speeds.

Playing with Your Food | 1 YEAR TO 12 YEARS

These games are perfect for fingers that are suspicious of anything that might be "yucky," as the novelty of food play can entice kids with tactile aversion. The goal is to become comfortable touching different textures—and what better way to experiment with touch than through play? Some of these games are also good for children with taste (gustatory) aversions.

Here are some fun games to play with food:

- **Digging for Worms.** Make mud out of chocolate pudding and crumbled cookies. Then throw in some gummy worms. This is not a healthy treat, but definitely a yucky one. If your tactile-sensitive child is willing to dig in the mud for worms, it's a good sign.

  If you want to keep sugar to a minimum, or your youngster is not quite ready for finger exploration, you can use coffee grounds for the mud and cups and spoons for a fill-'n'-dump activity.

- **Designs with Raisins.** Create raisin designs on a piece of toast with cream cheese by making shapes, numbers, or letters. If you do this ahead of time, family members can have the piece of toast for breakfast with their initials on it!

- **Eat Ants on a Log.** Fill a celery stick with cream cheese, and stick raisins in the cream cheese. Or use peanut butter for an even healthier combination. If

you want to change it up a bit, use assorted small dried fruit, such as cherries, cranberries, or currants.

- **Edible Play Dough.** Combine one cup of creamy peanut butter, two cups of powdered sugar, and a half cup of honey. Use cookie cutters to make fun shapes, or make your own shapes by hand.

- **Happy Faces.** Make smiley faces with food. If you are using vegetables, you can use carrot slices for the eyebrows, green pepper slices for the eyes, cauliflower for the nose, and bright-red pepper slices for the mouth. You can make an example or let your child's imagination be their guide. Just give a kid the ingredients for a fruit face, bacon-breakfast face, or vegetable face—and let the fun begin!

- **Paint with Spaghetti.** Cooked spaghetti is a little gooey, which makes it perfect for play. Cook some up, and run cold water on it to cool it; add a dab of oil, if needed, if you want to keep the strands separate. Then put tempera or any water-based paint on plates. Two or three colors are great, but one is enough.

    Have a piece of paper or shelf paper handy, and join your child in dipping the spaghetti into the paint and onto the paper for a Jackson Pollock original design! If you don't feel guilty about wasting food, pasta sauce or

pesto sauce can make wonderful "paint." Uncooked dry noodles can also be glued.

- **Broccoli Forest.** Cut up broccoli so they look like small baby trees. Design the ground out of peanut butter, stick in flowered spears, and you've got an edible forest!

- **Paint with Yogurt.** Mix plain yogurt with fruit juice, such as red beet juice, for a colorful and safe mixture. Your child can use a basting brush to paint their plate. For a larger work of art, use the mixture in the bathtub with a paintbrush, and your child can paint the tub red!

Texture Play | 2 YEARS TO 5 YEARS

If your child is hypersensitive to touch, you want to slowly diversify the textures that are tolerable and even fun to touch. Set a mirror on the table. While sitting together, pour a bit of powder or cornstarch on the mirror until you can no longer see your reflection. Then swish the dry material around until you see your eyes (or mouth or nose). Have your child take a turn experimenting with finding their own facial parts in the mirror by moving the powder or cornstarch to one side or another.

Once your child is comfortable with this dry material, up the challenge by using yogurt or whipped cream instead of dry powder, or even having a pudding party. In a pudding party, you can use large plates or you can cover the table with a plastic place mat or bag. Using store-bought or homemade pudding, put a glop in front of your child and another glop in front of you. Show your child how to spread it out like finger paint. And like finger painting, you can make unending designs and squiggles and

MODIFICATIONS FOR OLDER KIDS: You can slip some fine motor and academic skills into this game by drawing shapes or addition problems to solve. Make animal shapes, and have others guess what it is—or make fantasy animals. Use that spelling list from school or the dictionary and have a shaving-cream spelling bee!

finger marks, then swish them out with your hand and make a whole new one.

If you don't have any pudding, whipped cream might be a more appealing choice, or try mustard, ketchup, applesauce, or soy sauce, which are more colorful. Shaving cream is good for the kids who don't lick their fingers, and whipped cream better if they do!

Add sand to the preceding textures if you want to integrate even more textural input.

By experimenting with new textures, your child will learn to have fun with their hands. Don't be afraid to let their imagination soar!

Buried Treasures | 2 YEARS TO 10 YEARS

This game helps young children develop their tactile sensitivity and increase their tolerance for textures. For this game to be successful, use small items with distinctive shapes as the "buried treasure." Because this game uses many small pieces, always supervise your child, especially if they are still exploring objects with their mouth.

Fill a bowl with dried beans, rice, or macaroni and hide the "buried treasure" in it. I recommend plastic animal-shaped figurines you can find fairly cheaply at most toy stores. Try not to let your child peek while you hide the items—the element of surprise works well in this game.

The object is for them to use their hands to dig for buried treasures. Finding hidden things by touch is an exciting way of satisfying the tactile sense. The added excitement of getting a prize rewards children for using their desire for touch appropriately. Even the child who is learning to increase their tolerance for textures will enjoy this game.

Take turns reaching into the bowl and pulling something out. Ask, "What does it feel like?" "What did you get? A whale! Cool, my turn. Let's see what I got!"

After your child has enough experience reaching in the bowl and finding an object, increase their tolerance or satisfaction by putting the creatures in other materials. You could start with water that has lots of bubbles to hide the objects. Then move to more-challenging materials, such as cornstarch and sand.

Try using the following objects:

- comb
- clothespin
- coin
- button
- bracelet
- ring
- letters (refrigerator magnets)
- necklace
- barrette
- crayon
- shapes (parts from a shape-sorting box)

Add the element of searching by asking for a specific object: "Can you reach into the bowl and find the clothespin?" The child isn't then grabbing the first thing found, but instead has to dig through the bowl and feel for the desired objects.

If you're worried that your child might spill the bowl's contents all over the floor, you can still play this fun hunt by putting the treasures and the material (macaroni, rice, beans, cornstarch, and even sand) into a small paper bag or bucket.

MODIFICATIONS FOR OLDER KIDS: Coins can be used instead of toys. Detecting the difference between a dime and a penny can be just enough to distract children from the fact that they have their hand stuck in a bowl of sand—especially if they're allowed to keep the correctly gathered coins! If they can spell, use refrigerator magnets, and the first one to be able to construct a word wins!

If you have time to broaden the routine by bringing in action and language, you could have the animals talk and play with each other ("My kangaroo is going to jump over the hippo—what's yours going to do?") or line them up in size order for a parade.

Sock Game | 2 YEARS TO 10 YEARS

For children who tend to be undersensitive to their sense of touch, here is an easy game to play that will increase tactile awareness.

All you need is a big sock and common household items (for example, comb, key, ball, coins, paper clip, battery, dental floss, button, spoon, marker, eraser, pencil, small ball, chalk, crayon, barrette, or ribbon).

The simplest version is to put two things—such as a comb and a key—in a sock. You can tell your child what the two different objects are, and to reach in the sock—no peeking—and pull out the object named. You might say, "Can you put your hand inside the sock and, just using your hands to feel, pull out the one that is the key?"

A tougher version would be *not* to say what the objects are, and your child has to reach in, feel the object, and name it. You can also use more than two objects. Start off by making them feel very different from one another so they can be identified; then perhaps build up to more-similar objects (like chalk and a crayon, or a golf ball and a Ping-Pong ball).

To encourage children not to peek, ask them to close their eyes or feel inside the sock while it's held behind their backs. A scarf can be used for a blindfold. A paper bag over the head to keep eyes from peeking is another interesting and silly addition to the game!

To give children a sense of control and build their self-esteem, let them gather household items to put in a sock. Then, ask the child to present this game to family members, and let them guess what is in

the sock. The gathering of various materials is another tactile experience. If you want to control your child's choices, guide them to the drawer that contains objects for this game.

MODIFICATIONS FOR OLDER KIDS: Try hiding refrigerator-magnet letters in the sock, and see if they can identify the letters just by touch.

Back Drawing | 2 YEARS TO 10 YEARS

Drawing on a child's back with your finger is a fun way to help kids be more sensitive and alert to touch. This is especially true for hyposensitive kids who don't notice when they bang into things or hurt themselves.

The best thing is, you can play this game anytime—it requires no materials! Draw something on their back with your fingertip, and have them guess what it is.

Start with something easy, like a simple shape, and give clues. Say, "I'm going to draw a square or triangle on your back. See if you can tell what I'm drawing." Or, draw shapes on a piece of a paper—such as a star, circle, and diamond—and tell your child you will draw one of those shapes. Can your child tell which one?

To make it more challenging, draw a shape or letter without giving a clue beforehand. Try writing on other parts of the body, such as the arm or palm. Which is easier to feel? You can also take turns so your child gets to be the one in charge!

MODIFICATIONS FOR OLDER KIDS: Have your child sit down with a paper and pencil. Stand behind your child, write on their back with your fingertip, and have them write the letter they think is being written. If your child is old enough, use words to write a secret message! To make it part of a larger game, make the message a clue to where a treat or object is hidden. The word could be *microwave*, for example, where you've hidden a snack.

Games for Sight

The sense of vision is more than just about being able to see clearly. Our visual system also helps us see what we need to see and filter out what we don't need to focus on. Development of visual skills allows us to make sense of what we see in order to make judgments about the size, shape, and spatial relationships of objects. We begin to rely on visual skills for learning and organizing our environment.

Visual input can often be over stimulating for a child with sensory issues. If a child is hypersensitive to sight, she may be easily distracted or bothered by everything there is to look at. Conversely, a child may be hyposensitive to visual stimulation. This could be the child who doesn't seem to notice simple things, who seeks out bright, whirling, contrasting lights to fill her need for visual stimulation.

GOALS OF THE GAMES

We can help the over-responsive child by finding ways to simplify the visual field at home for a calming, organizing effect. This might include measures such as hiding clutter in bins and behind curtains. A solid-color curtain hung over a bookshelf instantly reduces visual clutter. A solid-colored rug and walls painted a soft color help put the eyes at ease, too.

We can also help these children with "I Spy" and "Where's Waldo"-type games, where they can hone their visual skills and practice attentive focusing.

Alternately, if the child seems tuned out and doesn't respond easily to visual stimulation, we can help by bringing visual attention to objects and things around him that he might not notice on his own. Activities such as going on a scavenger hunt involve having fun looking for things and getting rewarded.

We can also help the hypo-responsive child by using brightly colored objects to encourage visual attention. For example, a child who seems uninterested in watching a ball roll by may be more engaged if the ball lights up or makes noise as it moves.

Flashlight Game | 1 YEAR TO 5 YEARS

Two flashlights and a dark room make for instant fun. One person shines their flashlight on the wall, and the other player has to put their light on top of the other light. This can start off simply with one person moving their spotlight from place to place and the other has to join the spotlights together.

The fun can heat up when the element of chase is added and one person keeps moving his light here and there on the walls and the other has to keep up!

Take turns being the leader.

If another person wants to join the fun, add another flashlight and the game is guaranteed to be lively!

MODIFICATIONS FOR OLDER KIDS: Sitting in the dark, challenge your child and yourself to know where things are even if you can't see them. The challenge might be to shine your flashlight on something that starts with an *L* and your child lights up the laundry basket. An *M* might be the mirror. Roaming the room with the flashlight is the easy way; turning the spotlight instantly right on the objects is harder.

Which Cup Is It? | 1 YEAR TO 7 YEARS

 A classic carnival trick to capture someone's attention—and money—is to have three cans, and to place an object under one. The carny moves the cans around very quickly, and the player is supposed to guess which can is covering the valued object. When playing this game with your child, move slowly at first and encourage them to keep an eye on the correct cup.

Start with one small object and three identical paper cups. Place the three cups upside down on the table. Hide the object under one of the cups in full view of the child. Then move the cups around, however quickly seems appropriate, and stop and ask if your child knows which cup contains the coin underneath it.

Paying good attention to sight can even be rewarded with this game. Hide a coin under the cup, and if your player guesses which cup it's under, they get to keep the money! The game requires a child to watch closely, and this is what we want.

Foods such as fruit snacks are also good objects to use, because the child can eat it as a reward for answering correctly. Or you might use a special treasure, like a seashell or a marble, as a reward for each right answer.

Use more than three cups to enlarge choices, or only two to reduce choices. Let the child have a turn being the barker, and you have to guess.

For a young player, use cups that are different sizes or colors. Point out that the reward is being put under the red, not blue, cup. Then mix up the cups and see if your child can find the red cup and get the reward!

Cloud Pictures | 1 YEAR TO 12 YEARS

There isn't a one of us who hasn't seen figures in the clouds. Maybe a fluffy monster or maybe something more elaborate like a fanciful castle or a bird in flight? Sadly, though, once we grow up, most of us forget about this simple pleasure, so we rarely play it with our young ones, and it's such a wonderful way to encourage sight.

There is something satisfying about seeing shapes in the sky—say, a big bunny with perky long ears—and having someone else say that they see it, too! And if someone else also sees a silly dog with his tongue hanging out standing beside the bunny, you can add to the magic by making up stories: Where is that bunny going? Why is that doggie being silly? Where do they live? Where's their mom?

The next time you're outside or looking out the window together, you can turn cloud gazing into an "I Spy with My Little Eye" game. You can take turns looking at the whole sky and saying, "I see a dinosaur—who else can find it, too?"

Looking at clouds is a simple thing to do. But besides being a wonderful way to use vision, it's a good way to share attention in the moment with someone you love.

Cracker Box / Popsicle Stick Puzzles | 2 YEARS TO 7 YEARS

 Anyone who has put together a multiple-piece jigsaw puzzle knows how much depends upon using your sight to find the matching piece. You need to look at the colors, the design, and the protuberances of each piece to find the one that fits in exactly.

You can do a simpler version of a puzzle by making your own, and your child can help.

Cracker or cereal boxes are made of such nice heavy cardboard and already contain pictures and writing, so they are handy to use.

Cut out the front and backside of the box. Cut each side into two or more pieces, depending upon the skill level of your child. For very little ones, cut the front side in half and show how the two parts can be put together to make a whole picture again. Then let the child try completing the puzzle on their own. You can cut the backside of the box, too. This time use a diagonal cut so you have two triangular halves instead of two rectangles.

Let your child play with these pieces until it is easy for them to put the pieces together to make a whole picture. Then give the child all four pieces, and let them put the correct halves together.

For older children, cut the halves in half again so that there are now four pieces to each puzzle, or more if you wish. How many pieces you or your child make depends on his interest and ability to stay visually focused. Start easy and work your way up so the child is challenged but not overwhelmed.

If your kid is interested, try a professionally made box of jigsaw puzzles—this could become a lifetime hobby.

Or you could add a Popsicle stick puzzle to your child's repertoire. In this activity, you both use Popsicle sticks, craft sticks, or tongue depressors. You'll also need tape and felt-tip pens.

Lay four or five sticks next to one another as if making a raft. Then tape the sticks together on one side. Make two of them—one for you, one for your child. You both draw a picture using the pens or make a simple bold design that covers all or most of the untapped side of the "raft." Don't show each other your drawings. Next, untape the sticks and give the pieces to each other. Explain that you both should put the pieces together to re-form the picture that the other made.

Instead of drawing your own picture, paste a picture from a magazine on the sticks. Then separate the sticks with a sharp knife or scissors.

Up the challenge: Instead of using four or five sticks, use more to make a longer puzzle.

Share your Popsicle puzzles with other members of the family, and see if they can put them together!

Treasure Hunt | 2 YEARS TO 10 YEARS

 You know how entertaining Easter egg hunts can be. Finding hidden treasures is just plain fun, and it sharpens the visual sense. After all, you can't find a treasure if you don't look.

But there's no need to wait until spring to enjoy a good hunt. A bag of peanuts in their shells would work fine, or even small individually wrapped candies. Hide them around the house. Hide some in full view, and carefully hide others under something. If you want to spread the game across a bigger space, hide some outside.

You can also use written clues to help your child find the treasure. The clue could be "It's under something we all sit on together," or "It's under something blue."

If your child is allergic to peanuts, or you don't want your kid to have a sugar rush from candies, hide something else, such as stickers, or if they're old enough, marbles. At the end of the hunt,

MODIFICATIONS FOR OLDER KIDS: Up the challenge for bigger kids: Find tougher hiding spots, or use slips of paper—some blank, some featuring homemade "coupons" promising an extra hour before bedtime or an extra hour of computer time. You can also color-code the peanuts with markers and maybe invite some siblings or friends to join in: "Whoever finds the red one gets a candy bar," and "Whoever finds the most green ones picks the next game!"

found marbles could be combined together for a marble race: Flick them forward to see which one wins. Plastic animals, which are easily bought in bags at the store, can be hidden. Maybe the found creatures will inspire a zoo game. Poker chips might be fun to hide, and at the end of the game, players can make a large tower of chips together. Or roll the chips on their rims for a poker chip race.

But if the game just ends with a satisfying pile of peanuts to crack and eat, that is fun enough and a nice reward for playing a visual game.

Shadow Game | 2 YEARS TO 10 YEARS

 Next time you are outside with your young one, and the sun is low enough to cast a shadow on the sidewalk or ground, play this game. That's all you need—sun and a shadow!

Start by telling your child, "Whatever you do, *don't* step on my shadow." Telling children not to do something they really know is okay makes this game silly fun. So of course your young one will try and step on your shadow while you keep scurrying away, moving your shadow "out of harm's way."

When your shadow gets stepped on, switch roles. Now you can try and step on your fellow player's shadow while he tries to get out of the way.

You can get very specific if you want your child to be more exact with their vision by saying, "Don't step on my arm," or "Don't step on my chest." Now when you scurry around this way and that, the child will have to pay attention and notice exactly where your chest or arm is and quickly jump right on it.

You can introduce this more specific aspect of the game when it's your turn to step on your child's shadow. Say things like, "Which body parts should I *not* step on—heh-heh!"

This can be a game just between you two, to increase the ability to pay attention to sight. However, siblings can play along, too.

Even if players are inaccurate and step on the wrong part of the shadow, they are still having big fun with you, and that is something great, too.

I Notice Newness | 2 YEARS TO 10 YEARS

Let's say you are on a path or a street that you have walked on many times before, such as the path to school. Your child, however, is not in the mood to walk. Maybe they didn't sleep great, or is grumpy about leaving a toy at home. It doesn't matter what, right now—but it *does* matter that you get to school.

During those times, a distracting game can be a mood changer and a chance to hone those observational skills. Play the game of I Notice Newness. Look around and find something you hadn't noticed before. It could be a design around a door, or a face in the bark of a tree. Or maybe it is something that wasn't even there before: a flower that bloomed, a new sign.

Engage your child. Pique their interest. Does your child see the new thing, too? Give clues if needed. "It's blue," or "It's near the stop sign." When your child finds it, praise their clever eye, then challenge them to find something you hadn't noticed before. You can also bring in the spirit of competition and see who can find something new faster!

You can enlarge your child's language by giving sensory clues: "I notice something that's rough like sandpaper" or "I notice something that a bird would like to eat."

"I Notice Newness" can be a code phrase between you two for other days when you're walking that same path. The name will signal that the game has begun: Who can find something new fastest?

Your child is strengthening the ability to visually scan. On a physical level, scanning teaches control of the eye muscles, an important factor for good sight. On a psychological level, looking for and noticing new things increases your child's awareness of details. Today it's objects like a new flower or an architectural detail. Later, this same skill will allow your child to pick up nuances of facial features and body language.

And finally, emotionally, this game will distract your child from experiences that don't serve a good purpose. Instead of getting stuck on an annoying sensory aspect, such as the sound of a leaf blower, your child will be concentrating on visual information. Their attention will be on something pleasurable and the feeling of having fun with a parent. Maybe being even better than his parent at sighting new things will be the best reward of all. You can play this game with kids of any age—it makes for an easy way to get children to stay in the present moment. Use it on long walks, during long waits in airports, or car trips—in any situation that may feel overwhelming.

Magnifying Glass | 3 YEARS TO 10 YEARS

 I read somewhere that no respectable child should be without a magnifying glass in their life. That may be overstating the case, but I have given children a magnifying class on a string to wear around their neck when they are outside, and it has opened up exciting visual possibilities.

If children haven't used a magnifying glass before, they'll need some time to just play around with it and learn how to "make things bigger." You can then begin to focus the exploration. Find something that would be hard to see without the magnifier, such as the veins of a leaf or the patterns on your fingertips. Now look at these same things with a magnifying glass and see what other details suddenly open up. Does your child see something new with the magnifying glass?

You can take an exploratory hunt outside. Look at different things. Study the bark of trees, spiderwebs, parts of a flower, and bugs that are on the flower. An ant is a fascinating creature when seen large. Use descriptive language to talk about what's being observed. Use technical terms or observable ones. Bugs would have wings, antennae, and a thorax or perhaps be fat or tiny with lots of legs.

Or you could gather materials—such as different leaves, acorns, or shells—and bring them inside to study. The seeds of different plants are quite different and interesting to look at. For example, the nasturtium seed has many sides and looks different than the flower, while corn seeds look like popcorn.

Children are natural scientists. They like to explore differences. Your child may want to sort her findings by putting them in separate parts of a muffin tin; older kids may want to detail their findings in a journal or scrapbook.

The benefits of visual awareness are definitely brought out with a magnifying glass. Glasses can be bought at a toy or hobby store and come in different grades, from professional to a kid's toy.

You can even use a magnifying glass when looking for characters in a book. Your library probably has *Where's Waldo?* books. Waldo is a character who sets out on his journey equipped with 12 items to help him on his travels. As Waldo journeys from location to location, he loses one of these items, and the reader has to locate the object left behind in each scene as well. Readers are expected to scan the pages, but if you had a magnifying glass it would definitely come in handy!

Catch and Throw | 3 YEARS TO 12 YEARS

 Catching, throwing, hitting, and dribbling a ball all require the use of our eyes and our hands to be successful. That's why it's called eye-hand coordination. Our motor skills have to interact with our vision.

If you're working with a person who needs more practice with catching and throwing balls, there are advantages to some balls over others.

Beach balls, large and lightweight, are easier to catch than small balls. Foam balls can be easier to catch because they can be grasped. Beanbags can never roll away. Scarves give the catcher more time to make the catch.

If you don't have a ball handy, you can make your own. Scrunch up pages of newspaper into a ball shape, wrapping tape or cloth around it to keep that shape. Or put a few plastic bags into one bag, twist the top, and fasten in any way that keeps it closed and in a ball shape. Even place dried beans into the toe of a sock and knot the top.

There are many variations to this game:

- **Catch:** Your little players can practice catching by throwing themselves the ball. You can read out the instructions, and your player can follow your words:

  - Throw low, then throw high and catch with two hands.

- Throw the ball up and clap (once, twice, three times before catching.

- Start low and catch with one hand, alternating hands.

- Catch the ball underhand by letting it fall into a cupped hand.

- Catch the ball overhand by grabbing the falling ball out of the air.

- Put the ball on the backs of your hands. Toss it up and catch it.

- Catch the ball with one eye closed. Catch it with both eyes closed!

- Throw the ball up high, turn around in a circle, and catch it.

- **Tetherball:** Suspend a ball from a branch, and give your player a stick to hold horizontally. The child can take, say, 10 turns to hit the ball with the horizontal stick and see how many times it can be hit.

- **Dribble:** See how many times a ball can be dribbled. Start with the largest ball and work toward the smallest. For example, start with a basketball and work toward a tennis ball.

- **Partner catch:** Stand very close together and throw the ball back and forth. Every time a player successfully catches the ball, you both take a step backward, away from each other. Every time you miss and the throw or the catch didn't work, take a step toward each other. In this way, you will stay within the proximity of what works best!

Drawing What Matters | 3 YEARS TO 12 YEARS

Practicing drawing take vision and patience. But it's a wonderful way to focus attention and notice visual details. Try any or all of these:

- **Self-portraits:** Sit in front of a mirror with your child. You both have felt-tip pens. Trying not to move, draw the lines you see, starting with the shape of your head, then tracing your facial features, right on the mirror.

- **Family portraits:** Sit opposite your child and draw each other's faces on paper.

- **Personal things:** Invite your child to go around the house or their own room and draw objects that pique their interest. It may be a piece of jewelry, a favorite doll, or a small sculpture from a family vacation.

MODIFICATIONS FOR OLDER KIDS: Have your child write the story of how they received these special, personal things. Where did it happen, and with whom? Ask: "Why does it mean something to you?" This could be answered in a story, a video, or a comic strip—or, it could just be a lovely conversation you have with your precious child about some things that mean a lot to them.

Games for Balance

The vestibular system is found in the inner ear. It detects movement in the position of the head. If you've ever used a carpenter's level, you know that if the bubble is in the middle of the window, the board is level. The vestibular system is similar. There is liquid in the inner ear that acts like the bubble. We learn distinguish between when the liquid is centered and when it is not.

You can experience this sense right now: Close your eyes, and tilt your body to one side. You can probably feel, without looking, that you are off-center, and you know just which way to move to straighten up.

Children who are over-reactive or hypersensitive to vestibular stimulation may misinterpret the signal and believe they are in serious trouble, which can lead to a "fight, flight, or freeze" response. This feeling can cause them to be very frightened, run away, or even lash out. They might also have a fearful reaction to ordinary movements and shun playground equipment and elevator rides. They may even refuse to be picked up or let their feet leave the ground. And yes, they tend to fall often and may make a big fuss over a small fall.

Children who are under-reactive or hyposensitive to vestibular stimulation may purposefully seek excessive body movements; they are trying continuously to stimulate their vestibular system in order to achieve a state of quiet alertness. They will do activities to achieve this, such as whirling, jumping, spinning, hanging upside down, swinging for long periods or just constantly moving or fidgeting. And yes, they also tend to fall often, but may not even seem to notice or care.

GOALS OF THE GAMES

We want to help the children who are hypersensitive be aware of those feelings and test small experiences to become increasingly successful and less fearful. As children become more aware of their vestibular system, they become more adept at sensing and correcting imbalance.

We want the children who are hyposensitive to have those whirling, jumping, and otherwise moving experiences, but consciously—with their attention. Moving through an obstacle course, jumping while doing a 90-degree turn, hopping eight times, and so on, all add awareness to the movements.

Riding Boy / Riding Girl | 6 MONTHS TO 5 YEARS

 It's not unusual for children on the sensory spectrum to have "gravitational insecurity," which means they act frightened when their feet leave the ground. The vestibular system doesn't yet know how to read signals that tell the child she is okay even if off balance, and which way to move to get back into balance. Instead, kids with an underactive vestibular system might hear an SOS— alerting them that something is amiss about their balance, but they are not sure what to do about it.

Playing Riding Boy or Riding Girl gives them the experience they need to read these signals better. Bouncing a child on your lap is not a new idea, but for a child with vestibular weakness, it is the ideal game.

You sit in a chair, and your child sits on your lap, facing you. I sing these words, but you can sing anything you want:

Riding boy, riding boy,
Won't you be my riding boy?
Don't say no.
Here we go.
Ride awaaaay with me.

How vigorously or how slowly you bounce your child should be determined by watching their face. Start slow and speed up with the child's ability to adjust their balance.

Children often laugh loud and often as you go faster and faster, toss them to and fro, or bounce and sway. So do start slow, but don't be surprised if your child tolerates it well and wants more speed!

Ceiling Walk | 1 YEAR TO 3 YEARS

Ever walk on the ceiling? Every child lying on their back and watching a fly walk upside down on the ceiling must be envious. For the child who is fearful of being tipped, you can present this image of being a fly.

If you're feeling strong and a bit whimsical and are tall enough (that is key), you can make this image come true. If you are not tall, how about walking on the wall instead? If your child has an older sibling, perhaps do this with the older child first. This can provide the strength the younger child needs to get past their fears.

You can hold your child completely upside down, with their feet touching the ceiling, or just by their hips in a sitting position. Make sure you have a firm hold so you can both walk and your child will feel safe. Both you and your child take steps just as you do when walking. If your child is wall-walking instead, you can both sidestep. The game will be daring and fun enough, but if you want, you can sing "The Itsy Bitsy Spider."

Can You Keep
Your Balance? | 1 YEAR TO 5 YEARS

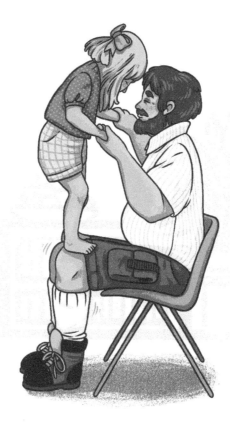

A fun and safe way for little ones to start practicing their balancing skills is to stand on your lap. The parent sits in a chair, while the child stands on the parent's thighs, holding onto their hands. When you sense your child is feeling secure and comfortable, begin to slightly jiggle your legs from side to side while singing a song. Any nursery rhyme will do, such as "The Itsy Bitsy

Spider." You can sing the regular lyrics, or you can sing about what you are doing. I like to sing to the tune of "Alouette":

Can you keep your balance?
Your balance, your balance.
Can you keep your balance,
Or will you fall down?

The point of this song is to add the joyful element of singing while you are doing something that has the element of a balancing challenge for your child. If younger or unable to stand, play the game with your child seated rather than standing.

As your child gets more and more secure, you can jiggle your legs more from side to side and even up and down. If your child gets more confident about keeping his balance, you can also try letting him hold on with only one hand!

This can be any parent's special game, or a grandparent, aunt, or partner can play it, too.

Afghan Ride | 1 YEAR TO 5 YEARS

 If you have a small blanket such as an afghan, or a large towel, you can give your child a fun ride that will work on their ability to understand balance.

Put the material on the floor. A wood or linoleum floor is best because it's more slippery and you can give your child a faster ride. But for the beginner or child who is especially fearful of movement, a carpet ride will do nicely.

Place your child on the material. She could at first be lying down but later work toward sitting up. Stand facing your child, and pull the end of the afghan or towel toward you as you walk backward around the room. A smooth, slow ride is good for the start, and it's always nice to accompany movement with song. Any song you want or even humming or singing "la-la-la" is perfect. You can see that this game can have a lot of variations:

- The ride could be jerky with lots of stops and starts.
- The ride could be whirly and go around in dizzying circles.
- The ride could be wavy and slowly go here and there around the room.
- Let the speed and intensity build or reduce according to your child's ability to tolerate being on and off balance.
- Take any siblings (or cousins!) along for the ride, or for a grand finale, sit on the blanket and let them pull *you* around!

Toads on the Path | 1 YEAR TO 7 YEARS

If you've got some old socks and some rice or sand, you can play this balance game. It helps kids deal with height in a fun way. The height in this case is no higher than a filled sock on the ground.

Fill up the socks—four or five would be good—with rice or sand.

If you want to make this game adorable, take a moment to make faces on the socks before you fill them. Call them "toads."

Lay the toads in a line and ask your player to do a variety of movements:

- Walk on top of them from one end to the other.
- Walk on top of them with your eyes closed.
- Jump over them one by one.
- Jump over them backward.
- Jump over them sideways.

If you have enough toads made, you might want to form a curved line instead. It makes balancing a tiny bit harder. Children have to adjust their balancing posture to adapt to the changes in direction.

And if your kid ends up picking up the toads and throwing them in frustration, don't fear. Throwing is another good coordination skill. You can gain control of the situation by pointing out a target: "Can you hit that post?"

Balance Beam | 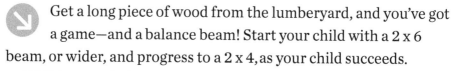 2 YEARS TO 12 YEARS

Get a long piece of wood from the lumberyard, and you've got a game—and a balance beam! Start your child with a 2 x 6 beam, or wider, and progress to a 2 x 4, as your child succeeds.

Walking on a balance beam placed on the floor can help children work on walking a narrow path and keeping their balance without real danger. Lay the board on the floor or yard, and ask your child to walk across the beam, the long way, without stepping off. The trick is to put one foot in front of the other—a toe/heel step. You might demonstrate what that looks like when you put your heel directly in front of the other toe to walk a straight line.

If your child has to step off a lot, take their hand to help them stay on the board. Later, work toward offering only a finger to hold on to, and then nothing! Also, praise them for stepping off less. "Why, you made it almost all the way only stepping off three times." If your child likes fantasy, pretend the beam is a bridge. I find that kids like it when I add, "Don't fall off, there are gators in there!"

To make it more challenging, place two large blocks or pieces of lumber under the beam to raise it off the ground, which will also give your child more experience jumping—jumping off the board!

> **MODIFICATIONS FOR OLDER KIDS:** Add more challenges to meet their skill level. For example, ask them to go backward while hopping on one foot or to cross the beam with their eyes closed while singing their favorite song.

We Are Rocking | 3 YEARS TO 7 YEARS

This is a game I play to help kids with their balance. Both feet are on the ground, but leaning to one side or the other helps children with SPD be aware of balancing while feeling secure.

I stand and begin to rock from side to side, without moving my feet. With the movement, I chant these words:

We are rocking, rocking rocking.
We are rocking, now we're still.

When I say the word "still," I hold my position, which is usually me leaning one way or the other. I hold it for a short while before I begin again. I might do this several more times trying to get the child to keep balance, even though the child is leaning to one side.

I then change my movement from side to side to back and forth. The weight now is shifting from my heels to my toes. I sing the same song, except this time when we stop, we are leaning forward or backward while trying to maintain our balance.

MODIFICATIONS FOR OLDER KIDS: Have the players stand on one foot when rocking side to side. This is a bit more advanced because on the words "Now we're still," they will have to hold their balance while standing on one foot.

Walking on Tape | 3 YEARS TO 7 YEARS

 You don't need to have a 2 x 4 board to play a balance game. A piece of masking tape will do. Put a piece of tape four or five feet long on the floor and have your child walk heel-to-toe trying to stay on the tape. Or put two pieces of tape down side by side two to four inches apart to make your own balance beam.

Walking on the "beam" (the tape or the space between the tape) without stepping off is a good skill. As children try to do more-difficult variations, they are gaining some insight to how to move their body to make it do what they want and learn that they are safe. These skills will then be transferred into other places and situations.

Once your child has accomplished walking across the beam easily, make new challenges:

- Can you walk forward and stay on the beam with one hand on your head?

- Can you walk forward with your arms straight up above your head?

- Can you walk forward with your arms crossed?

- Can you walk sideways with your arms on your hips and your right leg leading?

- Can you walk sideways with your arms on your hips and your left leg leading?

- Can you walk backward with your arms out to the sides, like a tightrope walker?

- Can you walk on tiptoes?

- Can you walk while carrying a tray so you can't see your feet?

- Can you walk while balancing an object on your head?

- Can you walk showing different emotions? Walk like you're mad. Walk like you're sad (and so on).

You could also say, "Show me a new way to walk across the beam, and I'll do it, too." Any activity is worth more esteem points if a parent does it, too!

Rocking Board | 3 YEARS TO 12 YEARS

Get a rock and a piece of lumber, and you can make your own rocking board. Place a 2 x 4 board or a strong small piece of plywood on a medium-size rock. If you're using the right materials, you should be able to stand on it and tilt it from one side to the other. And that is the game.

On the rocking board, your child gets their desired movement experience while practicing being aware of movement at the same time. Your child stands on the board and purposely tilts it from one

side to the other by moving their hips from side to side, alternately bending each leg to make the rocking board rock. The child will need to play around with it a little bit to get the feel of it.

Of course, I have a song to accompany this game. This song establishes a rhythm while giving instructions on what to do. Feel free to make up your own song and tune, or use mine. This song is sung to the tune of "Skip to My Lou":

Rock and rock and rock and roll.
Rock and rock and rock and roll.
Rock and rock and rock and roll.
Rock and roll and jump off!

Encourage your child to jump off the board when the "and jump off" words are sung.

If you're in a group, as each child stands on the board, direct them to follow these instructions. Then have all the children sing the preceding song along with whoever is taking a turn.

Games for Taste

The sense of taste is responsible for detecting all the different flavors that come into the mouth. Taste is perceived by our tongue, but how we interpret it is strongly influenced by our sense of smell. As an experiment, chew some gum until the flavor is gone, and then hold a lemon under your nose; the gum will taste like lemon.

Some children are hypersensitive and picky eaters, often with extreme preferences, such as a limited repertoire of foods or a resistance to trying new foods or restaurants, and may not eat at other people's houses. They may only eat "soft" or puréed foods or have difficulty with sucking, chewing, and swallowing.

Children with hyposensitivity of their gustatory sense may lick, taste, or chew on inedible objects, They sometimes prefer foods with intense flavor—that is, those that are excessively spicy, sweet, sour, or salty. They may frequently chew on their hair, shirt, or fingers, or constantly put objects in their mouth, well past the toddler years. Many also love vibrating toothbrushes!

GOALS OF THE GAMES

We can help children who are hypersensitive to tastes sharpen their attention to taste, which will enlarge their repertoire of acceptable foods. We can achieve this by involving them in food preparation, playing taste games where they identify flavors, and even playing with food!

We can help children who are hyposensitive to tastes by using their preference for strong tastes to stimulate the mouth in order to make them more aware of new foods.

We can also help by increasing the child's ability to suck and blow using games, such as using a straw to make a mass of bubbles or move a sticker. Giving them "chewelry" can also help by providing them with an acceptable object to chew. Companies like Stimtastic.co make silicone-based jewelry specifically for this purpose.

In essence, we help by making them more aware of their gustatory sense. This will help broaden the tastes they tolerate or like, or help arouse their sluggish gustatory systems.

Green Eggs and Ham | 2 YEARS TO 7 YEARS

Who has read *Green Eggs and Ham* by the incomparable Dr. Seuss? Sam-I-Am offers some green eggs and ham to a grown-up who refuses. Sam persistently tries to convince him to try it. "Would you eat it in a house, would you eat with a mouse? Would you eat it in a boat? Would you eat it with a goat?"

The fellow retorts, "Not in a house, not with a mouse, not in a boat or with a goat. Not here or there. Not anywhere!" This goes on verse after rhyming verse, until he finally gives up arguing and tries green eggs and ham. And, what do you know, he likes it!

This game entails not just reading the story, but acting it out. Who is Sam-I-Am, and who is the grown-up? Take turns trying both parts! The goal here is, you might help your picky eater see the humor in taking a bite of something previously not tried—and eureka, they may like it!

I Like It; I Don't Like It | 2 YEARS TO 10 YEARS

 Knowing your child's tolerance for different foods can help you decide if you want to expand their preferences or make them more aware of taste.

Start by making a chart. Make a big deal about this science experiment, in which the food is listed on the left and there are two columns, with a plus sign for "I like it" and a minus sign for "I don't like it."

Let your child be the one who is in control of the pen—your kid can make check marks in the "like" or "don't like" column, or put pluses and minus signs for each food item.

You can use the suggested food items listed under the What Is It? game (page 117) or buy special foods at the store, or just use whatever is familiar from your house.

Because you want to encourage your child to at least try a nibble on food, add a reward, such as stickers, for each food tried.

You could use coins, rewarding so many coins for each time the child tries a nibble on new foods, tastes, and textures. Or use points, rewarding so many points for trying out food and working toward a particular present.

Even if the child doesn't eat the new food, credit can be given for smelling it or licking it, or yes, even tasting it and spitting it out! All forms of trying something new get praised!

Remember to keep track of your child's food preferences. If it seems a child doesn't like mushy food, try apple slices and baked potatoes instead of applesauce and mashed potatoes. Or combine

mushy food with crunchy food; dip a cracker or piece of celery in the hummus, peanut butter, or salad dressing dip.

Notice if it's the shape of food that is significant. If the preference is for pizza, turn your quesadillas, bread slices, and lasagna into triangles!

Bread Faces | 2 YEARS TO 12 YEARS

If you have the time and interest, making bread from scratch is very enjoyable.

This activity works both your child's creativity and muscles! Start by adding yeast to warm water, and watch the bubbles form for your own little experience with chemistry. Next, add flour. This part is really good for children, as it is considered "heavy work"; it involves using the large muscles of the hand and arm. Keep stirring until the flour is thoroughly mixed in.

Then cover with a cloth and let the dough rise. Since this part can take an hour or more, it's a good time to give your child a reward for helping, such as watching a video or playing a game on the computer.

Once the bread has risen, break off small pieces and give one to your child. Show them how to knead the dough by folding it in half and in half again and again. Actually, there is no one right method, so let your child work the dough until they feel it get more and more elastic. If you have your own method, let your child imitate your style. If the dough feels goopy at first or anywhere along the process, just add more flour.

Next, make dough faces! Pat out a circular piece for the face, and break off smaller pieces for the eyes, nose, and mouth and add these to the face. You can make many faces with different features by making bigger noses, slanted eyebrows, and downturned mouths.

My kids and I used to also take large empty juice cans and squish some dough into the cans. The dough would rise in the oven and

form a rounded top. The lines on the can would be in the bread and show where to cut the bread into slices.

Put the face creations on a baking sheet and bake in a 350-degree oven for 45 to 60 minutes. Check every once in a while because smaller or larger pieces take different amounts of time—you don't want them to burn. What will be the same is the heavenly taste and smell of freshly baked bread.

Jaw Work | 2 YEARS TO 12 YEARS

Sometimes the problem with being a picky eater has nothing to do with the taste or texture of food. Sometimes the problem is weak jaw muscles. Maybe the muscles are weak because of genetics, or maybe your child has a habit of jaw clenching while sleeping and the muscles are tired.

If your child does this, or has bruxism (tooth grinding), you would want to check with a dentist. There are mouth guards that can be made or bought. It's not uncommon for any of us to clench our jaws at night when we are going through stress, so let your youngster know that it is not so unusual.

Like any muscle in the body, jaw muscles get stronger with exercise, and actually, the exercise in this case is chewy foods, really chewy stuff. Start with easy stuff, such as soft gum or Cracker Jacks, and work toward more chewy things, such as Laffy Taffy. Just as heavy work for the body leads to better overall fitness, heavy work for the jaw leads to better eating.

Needless to say, many chewy foods are sugary, so a good tooth-brushing should follow the chewing!

The following heavy-work foods help with jaw strength:

- bubblegum
- thick pretzels
- almonds
- large gumdrops
- chewy candy like Starburst
- frozen candy bars
- hard licorice
- whole carrots
- beef jerky
- granola
- fresh or stale bagels

- dried fruit
- caramel
- gummy bears
- taffy
- popcorn

The following skills also cultivate the jaw muscles:

- Sucking through a curly straw
- Sucking lollipops
- Drinking thick milk shakes with a thin straw
- Sucking hard candies
- Eating a spoonful of peanut butter
- Blowing bubbles in milk or juice with a straw
- Drinking Slurpees, applesauce, pudding, or something similar through a straw
- Sipping liquids through a sports-bottle cap

You can also prepare your child's mouth before eating by increasing stimulation as well as decreasing sensitivities in these ways:

- Have the child eat a frozen Popsicle made with real fruit to desensitize or increase awareness of flavors.

- Stroke your child's face with light finger touches, either yours or their own.

- Massage from underneath the jaw to the corners of the mouth.Instead of fingers, you can use a soft cloth to massage or stroke the face, jaw, and mouth.

- Hold a vibrating toy or toothbrush around, or in, the mouth. Vibration can also be very calming, soothing, and organizing.

- Have your child chew on rubber tubing, fish-tank tubing, or refrigerator tubing for several minutes before eating to get the jaws working.

- Use gum or "chewelry" to chew on for a while before eating.

- Massage your child's gums with your fingertips or use ARK's Z-Vibe, a vibratory oral motor tool that can help build oral tone. Its gentle vibration increases oral focus and draws more attention to the lips, tongue, cheeks, and jaw.

Musical Muscles | 2 YEARS TO 12 YEARS

 When we assess picky eaters, we always want to make sure the problem is not with the motor muscles of the mouth, lips, and tongue.

If a child can lick the ice cream around her mouth, suck through a straw, and blow a candle out, those mouth muscles are probably okay. But if there is any weakness or even if there isn't, here are some fun things to do to strengthen those muscles:

- **Play a kazoo.** A kazoo requires humming, and if you both have a kazoo, you can make beautiful humming together. Make your own kazoo by wrapping a piece of paper around a comb.

- **Toot a flute.** A recorder is the easiest version of a flute, and with just a little practice fingering the notes, your child could be ready to play "Happy Birthday" at the next event!

- **Play a harmonica.** Just sucking in and blowing out makes interesting sounds. Notes are numbered on the harmonica, so you both can also learn to play a tune.

- **Play your voice.** Make sounds, any sounds, and try and hold them as long as possible. Say, "ahhhhhhhhh."

- **Harmonize.** Try holding a different note from your child at the same time. Harmonize with funny words, like "hamburger" and "avocado."

- **Play with party blowers.** When you blow a party blower, the wiggly end extends. Can you do it 50 times in a row?

- **Compete with a paper-towel tube and Ping-Pong balls.** Can you have a Ping-Pong race and see who can blow through a paper-towel holder to make your ball go faster?

- **Play with pinwheels or pint-size windmills.** Make the blades go slow and fast.

- **Blow bubbles.** Children and adults never seem to get tired of seeing, chasing, or popping beautiful bubbles. Blow many little ones; blow one big one!

- **Get messy.** Compete with yogurt, pudding, or ice cream by smooshing it all around your lips and seeing who can lick their face clean faster.

- **Play with your tongue.** Can you make it go in and out like a snake? Can you make it go in circles? Can you curl it upside down?

Straw Play | 3 YEARS TO 10 YEARS

 Sometimes oral motor weakness is part of the reason children refuse certain foods. If their jaw muscles are weak, chewing meat can be too much trouble. Sometimes the muscles that control sucking and blowing are the ones that need reinforcing.

If you're working on sucking skills, this game will help. All you need are some stickers. Get a bunch of them beforehand, and lay them out on the table. Take two plain pieces of paper, and make five or more circles on each piece. The game is to suck through the straw and pick up a sticker and carry it to a circle. The person who gets their circles filled with stickers first is the winner. You might need to demonstrate how to suck on a straw to get the sticker to adhere to the bottom, and how to stop sucking in order to release the sticker.

If stickers are too hard to suck, use something easier, such as cotton balls. The idea is still the same: bringing in the spirit of competition to see who can fill their paper circles first.

Play around with different variations, or change the game on different days. Maybe another day the challenge is to suck up the cotton balls and drop them into a container, and the competition is about filling up your container before the other one does. Or cooperate and do it together!

Play with Your Food | 3 YEARS TO 12 YEARS

As children, many of us were told not to play with food. So it may seem counterintuitive to now suggest that if your child has a problem with food, she should play with it!

When working with food aversions, the goal is to be comfortable with food. Smashing it, rolling it, drawing on it, or making faces with food gives children time to touch food with their hands. Playing can take the mystery out of food and make it part of a regular routine.

Your child may not immediately put undesired food in her mouth because she played with it with her hands, but as time goes by, this familiarity can bring acceptance. The fingertips, like the mouth, are sensitive to touch. Beginning with fingers can help a child work toward the acceptance of different sensations in her mouth.

Here are some fun games to play with food:

- **Letters with Peas:** Give your child fresh pea pods. Encourage your child to hold the pod, to feel it, smell it, open it, count the peas inside, and if desired, to taste them.

  Make large letters on the tabletop with the pods. It's especially easy to spell *Mom* or *Dad* with pods. A child can get more elaborate and write their name using the small peas. Butter a piece of bread, and have them stick the peas to the buttered surface.

- **Eyedropper Cookies:** Make your favorite cookie recipe, but use eyedroppers or medicine droppers filled with cookie paint. To make paint, you could buy commercial icing or combine vanilla or lemon or any extracts with food coloring. Besides decorating, this is good for developing fine motor skills.

- **Vegetable Prints:** Zucchini, celery stalks, apples, and mushrooms are all good for making prints. Carrots and potatoes can be carved into specific shapes, such as a flower or star.

  Use hummus or applesauce, softened peanut butter, guacamole, or anything that inspires your child for paint, along with plates for the paper. Dip the vegetable in the sauce, and make an imprint on the plate. The design can be pretty enough to serve and delicious to eat.

- **Meatball on a Stick:** Use pretzel sticks, and have your child spear meatballs to make a new kind of shish kebab. If meatballs are not right, use grapes and raspberries, and alternate them to make a pretty pattern.

Describe It | 5 YEARS TO 12 YEARS

If you've played the What Is It? game (see opposite page) with your child, you can add to their awareness with this game about description. Sometimes it's hard to think of words to describe a food, so you can help by giving them words to choose from regarding the taste and the texture.

For kids who are sensitive, describing food can take away the mystery of troubling foods and answering questions makes it a bit like a science experiment! They might learn that they don't like crunchy foods in general, but certain crunchy foods aren't so bad.

Tell your child you want to play a new game: You will put a piece of food in their mouth while their eyes are closed, and they have to guess what the food is. Give them a small bite. Then ask either/or questions:

- Is it sweet, or sour?
- Is it tart?
- Is it salty, or not salty?

- Is it hot, or cold?
- Is it dry, or wet?
- Is it bitter, or tangy?

Ask questions about texture:

- Is it crunchy?
- Is it crispy?
- Is it sticky?

- Is it smooth?
- Is it chewy?
- Is it syrupy?

What Is It? |

Recognizing the taste of different foods is part of a child's path to developing discriminating taste buds.

For children who are hyposensitive to food, we want to increase their awareness of what they are eating by naming the food. To do this, take small pieces of familiar food and put it on a plate. Cover the plate with a paper napkin, or, best, blindfold your player.

If you can, start the game with another family member first so your child can see someone else, with blindfolded eyes, trying to guess the food that is in their mouth. You can bring the food to their nose to smell if they want.

Here are some possible foods, but use whatever is familiar in your house:

- peanut butter
- apple
- honey
- bread
- banana

- celery
- cucumbers
- cooked potato
- chocolate
- pear

- green pepper
- onion
- cracker
- spicy food

You could also include condiments:

- ketchup
- mustards
- gravy

- barbecue sauce
- soy sauce
- mayonnaise

- salad dressing
- spaghetti sauce

You can add to the excitement of the game by awarding points if they are right. You can do something basic by giving one point for each right answer. You can make it more fun by giving an outrageous number of points for correct answers. "You're right! That is cantaloupe, and you just got 4,300 points! Write that down!" Or you can award fewer points for "easy" foods, such as a mini-marshmallow, or more points for "challenging" foods, such as figs.

Ping-Pong Race | **5 YEARS TO 12 YEARS**

Children who are picky eaters because of weakness in the muscles that control the lips, tongue, and jaw can try this fun way to strengthen those muscles. Even if your child can blow, suck, and chew, these muscles could be reinforced—but in a novel way, of course—with a Ping-Pong Race. All that's required are straws and Ping-Pong balls.

Chalk out a starting line on one end of a table and a finish line at the other end. Mark your Ping-Pong balls with colored markers so you know whose balls are whose.

Place the competing balls on the starting line and get ready to blow them, through your straw, to the other line. If the balls blow off the table, you can gain more control if you race the balls in a shallow box with the goal to go from one end to the other.

If you don't have Ping-Pong balls, crumple small pieces of newspaper to about the same size and use them. Cotton balls wrapped with a bit of Scotch tape will roll well, too.

Blowing without the straw is fair play, too, and a little easier. If you want to make the game more cooperative than competitive, face each other and see if you can blow on your balls and crash them into each other!

Games for Smell

The sense of smell is our most powerful sense. Probably many of our oldest memories are associated with smells from when we were young, and in fact, this sense is fully functioning at birth.

The sense of smell is directly connected to the brain, and the brain perceives odors and accesses memories to remind us about people, places, or events associated with these olfactory sensations.

The sense of smell, just like the sense of taste, is a chemical sense: It detects chemicals in the environment. However, our sense of smell is dramatically stronger than our sense of taste. People can detect at least one trillion distinct scents. Our sense of smell is 10,000 times more sensitive than any other of our senses, and recognition of smell is immediate.

When odors enter the nose, they travel to the top of the nasal cavity to the olfactory cleft, where the nerves for smell are located. Other senses like touch and taste must travel through the body via neurons and the spinal cord before reaching the brain, whereas the olfactory response is immediate, extending directly to the brain. This is the only place where our central nervous system is directly exposed to the environment.

Children who are hypersensitive may react negatively to, or dislike, smells that do not usually bother or get noticed by other people. They might refuse to eat certain foods because of their smell or tell other people how bad or funny they smell.

The child who is hyposensitive may not notice odors that others usually complain about, or ignore or fail to notice unpleasant odors. They might make excessive use of smelling when introduced to objects, people, places, and food.

GOALS OF THE GAMES

We can help hypersensitive children by teaching strategies to use in intolerable situations, such as applying a lotion or cream that the child likes under the nostrils, or verbally preparing the child for smells she may encounter beforehand. Using oils and aromatherapy candles to provide a pleasurable smell and favorable reactions can also help.

The child with poor odor awareness and hyposensitivity needs to increase their sense of smell activities such as sensitizing their nose with smelling games. If your child likes to smell, try to provide appropriate opportunities, like in the kitchen.

Scent Bath and Scent Break | 2 YEARS TO 7 YEARS

 Vanilla and rose are generally calming scents, while peppermint and citrus are usually stirring. If your child needs help staying calm and loves vanilla, you can use a high-quality vanilla soap and bath oils at bath time. Let your child luxuriate in the smell and warm water. There are even candles that exude a vanilla scent that you could add to create a bath-time spa. There are also essential oils to put in an aromatherapy machine to produce calming smells.

Similarly, give your child a scent break. Sometimes, being at the grocery store or mall too long can be exhausting. If your child needs to be perked up, have a lemon handy. If calming is needed, rose lotion might be best.

In essence, if you know your child's favorite smells, bring them along when you are out. Avoid and anticipate a possible meltdown from sensory overload. Perhaps a cinnamon stick would be just the thing to distract and please your child. Or stop in a store that sells candles and soaps; your child can pick one out for a pick-me-up.

How Does It Smell? | 3 YEARS TO 10 YEARS

 Everything has a smell, or so it seems when we see children who like to smell everything. When they smell objects that don't appear to have an odor, we are curious as to why. When they smell food and reject it, we can understand it more. We know food has a smell, and the way things smell affect taste. There is a plethora of information about how smells influence taste. A common example is that someone smelling an apple can eat a potato and think it's an apple.

Our tendency is to tell children who smell everything *not* to smell everything. We might even tell them that it looks strange to other people (although we realize that what others think is not usually a deterrent).

There is a debate surrounding whether a child that likes to smell things does it because their sense of smell is underactive—and they are therefore trying to stimulate it by smelling everything. The alternative theory is that their sense of smell is over-reactive and very sensitive, and thus gives this child much more information than the other senses.

For this activity, it doesn't matter. What we ask them to do is give the object or food a judgment.

Based on your child's judgments, you can create a chart that says something smells good, stinky, or okay. The chart might look like this:

ITEM OR FOOD	JUDGMENT
car	good
couch	good
table	stinky
swing	okay

At the very least, this chart would give some information about why some things cause problems for our sensory child. Maybe the reason your kid won't sit at the wooden table is because it has absorbed many fragrances from many meals, and that is, to this child, extremely unpleasant, even if it has no odor to you. Maybe a tablecloth is all that is needed to hide those smells and get him to join the family at mealtime.

MODIFICATIONS FOR OLDER KIDS: Encourage older children to go beyond the idea that things smell "good" or "bad," and instead, ask them to describe the smell. If things fall into categories, use them. Categories can include "strong" or "weak," or they can be much more descriptive, like "mineral," "floral," or "earthy."

The Smelling Game | 3 YEARS TO 12 YEARS

If your child is averse to many smells, this game is good for finding out the most offending odors. By putting the scents directly under your child's nose, they can clearly tell you which ones are liked, disliked, and relatively neutral.

Prepare this game ahead of time by gathering up scents and putting a few drops on separate cotton balls, or grind or cut up some peels or herbs and put them in separate containers. Then you can present the scents, one by one, to your child. Write down each reaction. You might need to blindfold your child if it's obvious what the smells are by sight.

These are some scents that are fairly easy to find:

- vanilla extract
- lemon
- banana peels
- peppermint candy
- vinegar
- cinnamon
- rose petals
- orange skin
- clove

- rosemary
- thyme or other herbs
- grapefruit skin
- tea bags—get a variety
- perfume
- scented soap
- coffee grounds
- peanut butter

- jam (different flavors)
- garlic
- peppers
- pencils
- erasers
- white glue
- glue sticks
- grass
- dirt

If your child tends to be under-responsive to smells, this is an excellent game to sharpen the gustatory sense. You could do it in two ways: One would be, like in the preceding game, having the child just name the scent. The other would be having two containers or cotton balls with matching scents, and the game is to match them. Which one has the same smell as another?

Get the whole family involved. You might be surprised to find who has the sharpest nose!

Home Smells | 3 YEARS TO 12 YEARS

You can gather smells from around the house and put them in small paper bags. Or use socks, put items inside, and tie a knot in the open end.

Use items that are found around the house:

- orange peels
- onion skins
- potpourri
- herbs
- cut grass
- perfume

- peppermint candy
- lemon candy
- lemon
- licorice
- freshly made popcorn

- butter
- mayonnaise
- mustard
- ketchup
- soy sauce
- chocolate

One by one, present these to your child. If your child tends to not notice smell, see how many they can recognize. If the child is overly sensitive, see how many can be tolerated—but of course do not force your child to the point of discomfort.

It might work out better if your child has the fun of watching others try these scents first. This allows your child autonomy in this very fun game.

Markers, Play Dough, Scratch & Sniff | 3 YEARS TO 12 YEARS

You can buy markers or felt-tip pens that have a scent, although the scents aren't always accurate. Blueberries may not smell like the blueberries you buy in the store, so play this game a different way.

Name the flavors that the markers are supposed to have. One might be strawberry and the other bubblegum. Present two of the markers to your child, and give two choices. "Does this smell like strawberries, or bubblegum?" If your child guesses correctly, they get to keep the marker, and as an added reward, writes a large check mark on a piece of paper in that color.

Keep doing that by giving your child a choice of two markers. In the second round, give three choices: "Is this orange, blueberry, or grape?"

If you want to use play dough to smell instead, you can buy it or make your own, adding scented extract (lemon, vanilla, orange, and mint work well) to your favorite play dough recipe.

Or you can make your own scratch-and-sniff cards! First, mix a scent—such as cinnamon, cloves, vanilla, garlic powder, pencil shavings, soap, or essential oil—with a texture, such as sand, salt, or glitter. Paint some glue on a card, and pour on the scented texture. Make two cards of each scent so you have two sets. Let the cards dry, and shake off the excess.

Have the player and family members rub or scratch each of the cards and find the card with the matching scent.

Heat-Enhanced Smells | 3 YEARS TO 12 YEARS

 Heat can change the way things smell by increasing the level of scent. For example, raw cauliflower has a very faint smell, but cook it up and the smell is unique.

There are many types of aromatic lamps and candles that are used in aromatherapy that might be positive for your child and become part of their sensory diet.

Scents are known to enhance moods. For parents of a hyperactive child, it's intriguing to discover that a few drops of marjoram in their bath or vaporizer can have a calming effect.

Massage therapists sometimes use a particular scent when massaging a client. They often let each client choose the oils they prefer. Massaging a child with SPD, especially using a deep touch in which the muscles are firmly squeezed and the joints are compressed, can be very calming for them. Combining this satisfying touch with a favorite scent adds to the sensory experience. Lighting a scented candle can also help.

Don't overwhelm your child. Check in to see what scent or combination of scents is pleasant. Your favorite smells might not be the same as your kid's! If you are considering using heat to enhance a smell, check it out ahead of time. You can tell how an oil or candle smells when it is heated up by running a hair dryer over an object, so warm it up and see if your child likes the smell.

Vanilla might be a good massage lotion to start with for your child. It gives off a sweet, enticing aroma reminiscent of happy memories of home and childhood. It has a calming, relaxing, and comforting effect.

These Are a Few of My Favorite Smells | 5 YEARS TO 12 YEARS

A song from *The Sound of Music* reminds us there are favorite things we can remember when life throws us curveballs. We all have favorite smells. The smell of baking cookies is so enticing, sometimes realtors bake cookies when showing a house so potential buyers have a pleasant sensation.

What are you and your child's favorite smells? Make a chart ahead of time so your child can mark their opinion in one of three categories: pleasant, unpleasant, neutral. Checking things into categories makes a child feel respected and important.

Consider these smells and then add your own:

- freshly cut grass
- the outdoors after rain
- marshmallows roasting in an open fire
- laundry detergent
- burning wood
- wool sweater
- wet dog

- newly sharpened pencils
- glue
- baking bread
- bleach
- dirt when gardening
- favorite flower
- the ocean

What's the Memory? | 5 YEARS TO 12 YEARS

 When we are born, all our sensory systems are working, but what makes the sense of smell so strong is that the molecules that make up a scent go right into the membranes of our nose, so we have an immediate and lasting reaction to the scent. That's why we might smell something from our childhood and it still has a pleasant or unpleasant association.

In this game, you use whichever common or uncommon scents, such as the ones listed in the Smelling Game (page 125). As your player and you take a whiff, you talk about your memory of that smell.

Peanut butter might remind them of first eating their lunch in the school playground. Vanilla reminds them of a milk shake. Garlic, a local Italian restaurant. Association to smells is a unique experience, and you and your child might have very different memories.

You might be surprised at the memories that come forth when playing this game. You might even find that the smell that is so intolerable to your child has more to do with the association than the smell itself.

Remembering moments of the past together is a lovely and important way to spend time with your child.

What's Cooking? | 5 YEARS TO 12 YEARS

 Bringing your child into the kitchen while cooking is a logical way to increase their awareness of aromas. If you are frying up garlic in olive oil, it has a strong scent. You can prepare your child for the strong odor by talking about what you are doing while you are doing it: "First I'm heating the oil . . . Now I'm adding the chopped garlic . . . Now I'm stirring it around, and as I do that, the smell gets stronger."

There are ways to get your child involved in the cooking process. They can add ingredients that you give them or that they measure out. They can be the "sous chef" and cut up the vegetables or fruit, starting with something easy, such as cutting up a banana with a butter knife.

Letting your child take part in the cooking regime may not make the job go faster (though eventually, it might!), but it will add to their learning on different levels. There is a lot of math to be done by following a recipe that adds a teaspoon of this and a quarter cup of that. There are motor skills involved in stirring and cutting. There is visual stimulation when preparing a pretty plate. There are listening skills to be augmented by following directions. And of course, in cooking there are a variety of aromas to stimulate the olfactory sense.

Outdoor Smells | 7 YEARS TO 12 YEARS

 When we go outside, whether we live in the country or in the heart of a busy city, there is a range of identifiable and not-so-identifiable smells.

Sometimes we forget to just take a sniff and see what is in the air. What is that smell? Where is it coming from? Is it pleasant? Is it stinky? Is it odd, or very familiar?

Encourage your child to track down a smell. That smoky smell? It turns out to be a neighbor burning fall leaves. That oily smell? It's from the fast food restaurant. This detective work helps a child who is sensitive to smells know exactly which smells are bothersome and where they come from—if only to know what kinds of places to avoid!

You might bring in other senses. Can you hear a smell, such as a cement mixer mixing a batch of cement for the new sidewalks? Can you touch a smell, such as the petals of a rose? Can you taste the smell of French fries?

If there are things your child would like to smell more of, is it possible to collect outdoor items, such as tree bark, acorns, and simple herbs, and bring them into the house? You can also buy fragrant herbs at the plant store and place them on the kitchen windowsill. They are inexpensive and add the elements of touch and taste to this sensory experience.

Games for Movement

There are small receptors within our muscles and joints, ligaments, tendons, and connective tissues that detect the amount of stretch that occurs. Our awareness of these receptors allows us to sense the movement of our body parts without having to look at where they are. It could be considered the "position sense."

You can test this sense right now by closing your eyes and putting your arms straight out and even moving them in and out. Without looking, you know exactly what your arms are doing. Your proprioceptive sense tells you.

A child who is hypersensitive to the sense of movement may be a super athlete, but the opposite is true for the child who is hyposensitive. Without proper messages about movement, children will have signs of proprioceptive dysfunction. They might be kids who are clumsy, uncoordinated, and have difficulty figuring out how to make their bodies move certain ways. They may trip and fall often. Not being able to listen to the proprioceptive sense might show itself through difficulty regulating pressure when writing or drawing, and they may push too light or so hard that the pencil tip breaks, or rip the paper when erasing. Some may do everything with too much force, stomping their feet while walking and slamming doors.

These children often seek more stimulation by actively craving more sensory input. They may seem to have an almost insatiable desire for sensory input, and be constantly moving, crashing, bumping, or jumping. Sensory seekers are often thought to have ADHD because these desires can cause children to behave as if they are impulsive, angry, disobedient, or difficult to control.

FIDGETING

In her article, "The Real Reason Why Kids Fidget—And What We Can Do about It," pediatric occupational therapist Angela Hanscom writes, "Fidgeting is a real problem. It is a strong indicator that children are not getting enough movement throughout the day. We need to fix the underlying issue. Recess times need to be extended, and kids should be playing outside as soon as they get home from school. Twenty minutes of movement a day is not enough! They need hours of play outdoors in order to establish a healthy sensory system and to support higher-level attention and learning in the classroom. . . . In order for children to learn, they need to be able to pay attention. In order for them to pay attention, we need to let them move."

GOALS OF THE GAMES

Ironically, for children, the result of all their excess movement (although sometimes disruptive to others) is calming to them. One way we can help a child stimulate their proprioceptive sense and the resultant calmness by engaging in activities that push joints together, such as pushing something heavy). Another way is to engage them in activities that that pull joints apart, such as hanging from monkey bars; carrying a trash can, box, or laundry basket; jumping on a trampoline; jump-roping; sweeping the floor; raking leaves; or digging in the garden. These are all examples of "heavy work" that can be done at home (see more heavy-work ideas in Appendix B). Heavy work uses muscle and stimulates the proprioceptive and vestibular systems, two major sensory pathways.

We can also help calm their sensory-seeking system with activities that involve deep touch, such as cocooning—when we wrap a child up tightly in a blanket or large towel, or when we give them strong bear hugs or deep massage.

We can also help the child who is uncoordinated by increasing their gross motor skills. Helpful activities like ball catching and broomstick jumping teach them how to move their bodies in specific ways. By enhancing their motor skills, it makes it more possible for them to join in the play at recess with the other kids.

And when school is over, you can add additional activities to their life that may be available in your area, such as swimming, horseback riding, and bowling.

Creating ways to incorporate these needs into safe and fun activities that provide the desired intensity fulfills their needs and may allow your child to come to a calm and focused place.

When they are in situations (such as a classroom) where jumping and crashing is not allowed, there are ways to modify their positioning, such as letting them sit on a slightly inflated beach ball or air cushion so they can sit and still move. Tying a thick rubber band on the legs of a school chair can give restless legs something to push against to feel calmer and pay attention.

Boat Box | 1 YEAR TO 5 YEARS

 A cardboard box from the grocery store is the perfect thing to turn into a boat. Set up the story ahead of time: "We're in the middle of the ocean [if she knows an ocean or body of water, use that name], and we want to go to Grandma's house [or use another familiar and loving person]. Let's go and get in our boat!"

Place the child into the boat box, or let her climb into it, and if you want to add extra comfort, tuck a blanket or pillow in the box around them. Sit down beside the box, and while singing a song such as "Row, Row, Row Your Boat," gently rock the box from side to side. Keep this going for as long as your child likes it and you have the time to play.

When you feel your child is ready to increase the level of fun (and balancing), you can say, "Uh-oh. A storm is coming!" and start to shake and rock the boat box more vigorously. The storm can get worse and worse, then better and better until it's all calm and quiet again, and you can praise your child's bravery.

At some point in the storm, if you are both willing, tip the box over to let her fall gently out. Pretend to make a big deal about the boat capsizing—"Oh no! We have to fix the boat!"—and let the child help you right the boat and get back in, and sweetly rock away again: "Merrily, merrily, merrily, merrily. Life is but a dream."

The Way We Wash/
Monster Mash | 1 YEAR TO 5 YEARS

 Why say it when you can sing it? Every day there are things to get done, and one of them is getting one's body washed. If your kid is reluctant to be touched, you can sometimes get more mileage if you sing *specifically* about what you're doing, while you're doing it. For example, try singing to the tune of "Here We Go, Round the Mulberry Bush":

This is the way we wash your forehead,
Wash your cheeks, and wash your chin.
This is the way we wash your face,
Every single day.

If you talk about each part, your child will stop for a moment and feel that chin that you're singing about, from the inside. That is what listening to your proprioceptive system looks like.

When giving a bath, sing about all the body parts as they are scrubbed. You might choose to use your hand or something else, such as a washrag, small surgical brush, infant hairbrush, or nylon net.

This playful and musical game can also help children decrease their sensitivity to tactile input.

The Monster Mash game can be played afterward when you're drying your child with a towel. First, tell the child you are going to pretend to be a "monster" so they don't get scared! Then, put a towel down on the floor or changing table. Ask your child to lay on their belly, then cover their back with another towel. Then, using your hands and starting at the feet, firmly squish their body through the towel as if you were crawling up from feet to shoulders, making appropriately monster-like growls!

The Kid in My Lap | 1 YEAR TO 5 YEARS

 Chances are the child seeking sensory input will be seeking it all over you, climbing on your back, jumping in your arms (even if you aren't prepared for it!) and sitting in your lap. You can provide a good dose of sensory input and have fun together at the same time with this game.

Do you know the song about the bus? It starts off with "The wheels on the bus go round and round, round and round, round and round. The wheels on the bus go round and round, all through the town." In this game, you change the words to be all about your child: "The kid [or name] in my lap goes up and down, up and down, up and down. The kid in my lap goes up and down, all day long."

This activity is so great because the modifications and variations are endless. For the sensory-timid child, you croon the tune while gently providing that little bounce. You can also enlarge a child's tolerance for movement by jiggling a little faster or adding variation, such as going side to side. As your child gets braver, lower their head so it's upside down, while holding firmly on to their hands and singing the end words, "all day long."

For the sensory seeker, go nuts. Start slow, and then give them all the bouncing they desire. Up and down and side to side. Go fast, go slow, and keep changing the rhythm for surprise—because the child won't know when you are going to suddenly speed up again. You can make a surprise finale by suddenly opening your legs and have your child "fall through." No worries, you still are holding hands!

Hot Dog with Cushions
& Pickle Sandwich | 1 YEAR TO 7 YEARS

Pretending to be a hot dog or part of a sandwich may not seem appealingto you, but your sensory-seeking child will enjoy the calming hug-like sensation.

HOT DOG WITH CUSHIONS

Tell your child to lie down on a sofa cushion—right in the center. Then say that you like mustard on your hot dog, and rub them vigorously all over with imaginary mustards. Like relish? Want ketchup, too? Keep going until your "hot dog" is smothered in the pretend condiments.

Now it's time for the top bun. Take another sofa cushion, put it on top of the "hot dog," and push down. Your child is now lying in between two cushions, and this little hot dog is nice and snug. Ask, "Do you want me to squeeze more?" "Should I press harder or softer?" You might be surprised how much your child delights in this and may want even more pressure.

Author and professor Temple Grandin, who has written a lot about her autistic life, even invented a "squeeze machine" to could get just that kind of effect. It's calming and satisfying in just the way a strong hug can be, but without the social obligation to hug back.

PICKLE SANDWICH

If you want to make this a social thing with siblings or neighbors, you can get the same results with several children by making a "pickle sandwich." In this game, the children are standing. Two children are the bread slices and face each other; the one in the middle is the pickle. You put your arms around them all, pull them tightly together while they giggle, squirm, and laugh, then pretend to eat your sandwich. Yum yum. What could be better than a delicious pickle sandwich?

Sushi Roll and Hammock Swings | 2 YEARS TO 7 YEARS

Both of these games are traditional in that they are routinely used to stimulate the proprioceptive system—the movement sense—and even though they involve being wrapped up and rolled out, they are calming to the child with sensory differences.

SUSHI ROLL

Whether you call this game Sushi Roll or Burrito Snack, the idea is the same, and it's a classic way to give sensory seekers, and all children, the sensation of being hugged.

Lay a blanket on the floor, and have your child lie down horizontal to the bottom edge of the blanket. Then roll the child up in the blanket as if rolling up a sushi roll or burrito. If your child invites more input, you can push down on the bundle as if you were squishing it all together.

Once rolled up, you can pretend to eat the yummy treat. After your snack, lift up one edge of the blanket, and unroll the child by lifting up on the blanket until they are rolled free.

HAMMOCK SWING ROCK AND ROLL

You need another adult for this game. A blanket is folded in half, and each adult holds one end of the blanket. Your child lies down on the blanket as if it were a hammock. The adults pick up the blanket and rock the child back and forth, chanting these words:

Rock and rock and rock and rock!
Rock and rock and roll!

At the end of the chant, on the word "roll," the adults tilt the blanket close to the floor and let the child roll out. Ideally, they keep rolling and rolling just for the fun of it. Be sure that you have a soft floor covering for this game!

Other activities that are similar and also calming to your child are being wrapped up in a blanket, being rocked very slowly, getting a big bear hug, snuggling in a big comfy chair, firmly squishing legs and arm with a pillow or exercise ball, sleeping under a weighted blanket or heavy quilt, and even taking a warm bath.

Ropes That Swing and Snakes That Wiggle | 2 YEARS TO 10 YEARS

This game is for children who are not yet ready for the traditional game of jumping rope, where the rope goes over their heads. In this one, the rope is gently swung from side to side, not in a full circle. You don't need two people to hold the ends of the rope. Just tie one end to a table leg or anything appropriate.

Have your child swing the rope so you can demonstrate how to jump over it at the correct time. Show how the idea is to jump when the rope is near and not when it is swung away. Children learn to time their jumps to go over the rope when it is swung near them.

How slowly or quickly the rope swings depends on the child. For the beginner, you would want to swing the rope gently until they get the idea of when to jump. You can give verbal cues such as "Ready . . . set . . . jump!" You can increase the intensity as the game progresses.

Your hyperactive child may want you to go faster, but the challenge of rhythm and timing will teach that slowing down and paying attention will better serve them in the long run.

SNAKES THAT WIGGLE

If you have a long scarf, a woven belt, or a piece of rope, this is a fun game children love that works on balancing skills.

Hold the rope (or belt or scarf or whatever) by one end. Wiggle that end so the rope wiggles on the ground like a snake. Keep the

rope touching the ground when you are wiggling it from side to side so it will stay harmless.

As you wiggle it, say, "I bet you can't step on this!" or whatever words would motivate your child. Their job is to try and step on the rope so you can't move it. In the snake version of the game, your kid must try to step on the head of the snake so it can't bite them!

Start easy so the child has the experience of being successful and stepping on the rope. You can pretend to be flummoxed or upset that your kid was able to stop your movement. I find that kids get a kick out of being able to "outsmart" grown-ups. After the child stops the rope, have them step off the "snake's head" so the two of you can start again.

This is a fun game to play with a lot of kids, so definitely let siblings, cousins, or neighbors join in if they are there.

You can let a child have a turn wiggling the snake, but my experience shows that kids tend to get excited and swing the rope above the ground rather than touching the ground. That can hurt!

The Countdown | 2 YEARS TO 10 YEARS

With this one game, you can tire a child out, calm their system, and take advantage of their need to move. This game is so simple that you will be surprised at how many times you can use it or how such a simple approach could be so effective, but I promise it works well. I have tried it with all ages and skill levels and attitudes, with equal success.

It goes like this: "Let's see if you can run upstairs, get your shoes, and be back downstairs before I get to the number seven. Ready? Set? Go! One . . . two . . . three . . . four . . . five . . . six . . . Good! You made it by six!"

Please note that this approach is quite the opposite from the old threat, "I'll give you to 10 to get those shoes, or you know what!" This is a positive game of challenge and speed that you could some- times play just to use up excess energy before dinner or while waiting for the school bus. "Let's see how fast you can run around the tree and touch the rock and come back. Ready? Set? Go!" Use a stopwatch, and if your child is up for it, see if they can repeat the challenge and beat their own time.

I have also used a timer, as in "Let's see if you can get your toys put away before the bell rings!" Although if the job is overwhelming, I might have to say instead, "Let's see how fast *we* can . . ." and enter into the spirit of it. (I notice that if my job is to pick up all the dirty clothes and put them in the laundry basket by the count of 10, it's more fun for me to do, too.)

My children showed me that this game can be done to help one's emotional state. One day I was driving home from a long trip. It was rainy and dark, the road long and winding. The children had been cranky and fussy for a long while, and I wasn't feeling much better myself. I finally blew up at them to "Be quiet!" (or something similar).

The oldest child, then five years old, said serenely to me, "Do you think you could calm down by the time I count to seven?" She began counting, "One . . . two . . ." When I realized that she was playing my game on me, my lips curled up in amusement. She said, "Good job! You did it by six!"

> **MODIFICATIONS FOR OLDER KIDS:** A stopwatch has the added advantage of teaching mathematical concepts, such as which number is bigger: "Look, you swept the floor perfectly, and you did it in 2 minutes and 49.6 seconds. That's 12 seconds less than yesterday! Let's make a chart and see if you can beat your top score tomorrow."

Shoe Mountain | 2 YEARS TO 12 YEARS

When your child has too much energy or is just about unable to contain that energy, jumping is always a good bet. It brings the focus back into the body and satisfies the need for sensation.

What to do right now? Since everyone has shoes in their house—often cluttering the entryway—you can put them to good use in the Shoe Mountain jumping game.

Start off with a small challenge. Put two or more shoes on the floor and ask, "Can you jump over these shoes?" You might enhance the challenge by adding ". . . as easily as I do." Children sometimes get a thrill out of besting their parents. If there is another sibling present, better yet.

Then add another, "Can you do three?" Keep adding a shoe to the line and see how many he or they can jump over. If you want to add more challenges, ask your players to jump sideways or backward or even add a twirl in the air before landing!

Then pile the whole bunch of shoes on one end of the room. Announce that this pile is "Shoe Mountain." The game is to start running from one end of the room toward the mountain and, when they get there, leap over it! You could do a demonstration first of running and leaping.

Make sure, of course, there is room to land on the other side of the mountain so nobody bangs into the wall! You can also add to their joy of leaping by doing a drumroll. Add drum sounds by slapping your thighs or clapping your hands while your child is running. Then, as your child makes the grand leap, shout out their name! All children love hearing their name yelled out.

Monster Chase | 3 YEARS TO 7 YEARS

It's not a good day! Your child, who can be so sweet, is being obnoxious, dictatorial, mean-spirited, and dare I say, spoiled and bratty! You don't know why. The child probably doesn't know, either, but what's worse is that you, the normally sweet parent, is furious—thinking thoughts you'd never in a million years act on, but still this kid is ruining your self-concept and your day. You're the nice, loving, calm parent. What to do?

Release those monstrous feelings you are having, in a friendly way. Play the game of Monster Chase.

Start off with a loud growl to get the child's attention, and then say, "I'm an ugly, mean monster, and I'm going to get you! You better run!" Then, making monster sounds, use your mad energy and chase that kid all over the house and up and down the stairs and all around the backyard, up the stairs again.

If you catch the child, turn into the Tickle Monster. Not the light, annoying tickle, but the deeply felt, satisfying kind. Let the child easily get away, and then start the chase again. Repeat until you are both exhausted. Then, both tired, you can cuddle awhile or have a snack and start the day over again, in a much better mood. Maybe in that state you can talk about feelings and what set him off earlier or not. But no matter what, that bad moment was changed into a fun one—the game was a game changer.

Look, we all get in bad or sad moods. It's part of the human condition. But how long we stay in one and how we get out of one is a learned skill. Children with SPD can have difficulty with changing directions and may get stuck in a feeling or mood. By experiencing this game of chase, they learn that movement can be a way out of a bad mood. They will use this awareness all their life. Maybe they'll use it when they are older, and know to go for a walk to cool down when they are angry. Maybe as adults they'll learn that going for a run first thing in the morning sets them up for a calmer day. Mainly, they learn that moving their bodies is a positive thing. But what is even more important at this stage in their life is learning that their parent loves them enough to deal with their own bad mood by having fun with them!

Broomstick Game | 3 YEARS TO 10 YEARS

 If you've got a broomstick handy, you've got an enchanting game for young kids who love to jump. For a child who wants movement and lots of it, this is ideal because it allows movement but requires focusing. You'll also be working on their ability to stay balanced and work their large muscles.

"Want to play the Broomstick Game?" is a good way to begin, because no one has any idea what that is, and even reluctant players are curious.

You show them by first laying the broomstick on the ground and saying, "Can you jump over that?" Once they show you how easy that was, and maybe even laugh at you for suggesting something so simple, you begin to up the ante:

- Can you jump over it on one foot?
- Can you do it with the other foot?
- What about jumping over sideways?
- Can you jump sideways, facing the other way?
- Can you do it backward?
- Backward on one foot?

Once your child has accomplished all those movements—or tried for some approximation of those movements (and trying counts for a lot)—you can challenge them even more. Raise the broomstick up a smidgen and ask them to jump over this new height. Once your child can do that a few times, add any or all the variations. If you want to get fancy, you or your child can make up your own silly variations, like, "Can you jump back and forth while counting to 10 and waving your arms?"

You can also keep raising the broomstick so it's higher and higher. You definitely don't want your child to trip over it, so only go as high as it remains a fun challenge.

Games for Sound

Hearing is a mechanical process. We have the ability to perceive sound by detecting vibrations through the ear. Ears convert sound waves into nerve impulses that are sent to the brain. These nerve impulses are what the brain interprets. While your ears pick up the sound, it is your brain that does the work of making sense of it all. Our brain determines which sounds are important. Is this a sound that has meaning in my life, or can I ignore it? Is that the sound of an ambulance siren, or a bird chirping? Is that person crying? Do I hear the sound of cellophane crinkling as a piece of candy is being unwrapped?

The auditory sense also helps us locate where sounds are coming from. Is it behind me, beside me, close, or far away? All important details. In fact, we depend on our auditory system for survival, and if the auditory information is not processing properly, it can be overwhelming and disorienting.

From a sensory-processing viewpoint, children who seem upset a lot might be so because of the continual sensory overload. It could be the loud sounds of the urban environment or the sounds most of us either don't notice or become used to, such as fans, clocks, refrigerators, or outside traffic.

As a consequence of this overload, the nervous system can perceive danger, and a fight (rages, tantrums) or flight (withdrawal, shutting down) response or freeze response may occur.

On the other hand, you may see a child with a hyposensitive auditory system seeking out loud noises. This child may demonstrate difficulty localizing and distinguishing sounds or responding to their name being called, or needs you to repeat yourself often, doesn't seem to understand what you said, or is unable to recognize where sound is coming from.

GOALS OF THE GAMES

We can help children with hypersensitivity to sound by bringing purposeful attention to the auditory system. Name those sounds they hear. Figure out where are they coming from. What can be done right now to deal with an unwanted sound? When children are aware of what is bothersome, learning their own strategies help give them control over the amount of sensory input they have to deal with, such as using noise-cancelling or noise-minimizing headphones, iPods to play soothing music, earplugs to dull sounds, taking regular hearing breaks in the quiet of the bathroom, or singing aloud!

We can help children who are hyposensitive to sound by giving them many experiences in identifying sounds and finding the pleasure in learning to listen. We can also do helpful things such as having them repeat back instructions before beginning a task. We could use visual directions along with auditory, such as sign-language gestures or photos.

Children who have problems with the mechanics of hearing might have an auditory-processing disorder (APD). These symptoms can sometimes overlap, and so a speech pathologist can work on improving their skills in distinguishing, remembering, and sequencing sounds.

The games in this chapter help children increase their awareness of sound. They give your child some control, whether it's by making their own music or learning to listen to the neighborhood birds.

Who Am I?
and What Is This? | 2 YEARS TO 10 YEARS

Make up a list of clues about someone or something your child knows. Your child's job is to listen to all the clues and figure out who or what you are talking about. Remember to include things as well as people.

A people cue could be about a favorite uncle: "He is very tall with a dark mustache, and he always gives you a high five!"

A harder cue would be about an object such as a lamp: "This is something that lives in the living room, and we always like to use it at a certain time of day. If it's not the right time, we just ignore it. It goes on or off whenever we want."

Who Am I? is a great game to play with different ages because the clues can be very simple: "This is a person who loves you and snuggles you every night when you go to bed." (A parent!) Or they can be difficult and cryptic: "This is a magic person who only comes in the night, and she takes something and leaves something." (The tooth fairy!).

No matter who the player is, it takes good listening to hear the clues, remember them, and put them together with a memory. One of the best things about this game is that it can be played anywhere. If your child is getting fussy while waiting at the dentist or waiting in line or riding in the car, bring on the Who Am I? game.

WHAT IS THIS?

Your child closes their eyes, and you knock on something using your knuckles or a spoon. The game is to have the child guess the item you are rapping on. Knocking on a refrigerator will have a different sound than knocking on the table. Ask your child to guess what you are knocking on. Give choices if the sounds are hard to distinguish. "Am I knocking on the window, or the drinking glass?" "Am I knocking on the table, or the stove?" You can also make sure the items are very different from each other; for example, metal and glass when knocked on don't sound at all the same.

Some children will do well with a scarf over their eyes or a paper bag over their head to make them not peek. You can take the blindfolded child from room to room, knocking on different items, which prolongs the fun. Other children would do better if they just turned their backs and were encouraged not to cheat and peek when they came into a new area.

MODIFICATIONS FOR OLDER KIDS: Present an older child with more-difficult clues, and then they have to ask a series of yes-or-no questions to narrow down their guesses to the correct answer. "Do I know him?" "Is it electric?" "Is she famous?" An older child would also enjoy making up clues for a younger sibling.

A variation on this game would be to make sounds with household objects. An eggbeater has its own sound, as do two pot lids banged together, keys on a ring, the ring on a timer, and a cheese grate being strummed by a spoon. Look around the house to notice what makes a distinguishing noise.

Another variation would be to gather up some musical instruments, such as a xylophone, harmonica, bells, drum, guitar, ukulele, or whatever you happen to have in your house—the more

specialized the better—and put them in a basket. Your child has to guess each item you take out of the basket by the sound it makes.

If you want to make your own version of sounds, you can use salt, rice, popcorn, buttons, gravel, beans, sand, and pennies. Each material should be poured into small bags or containers and shaken to identify the sound. If you make two versions of each, your player could find the matching sounds and pair them up.

Play these games more than once so your player gets a chance to learn the differences in sounds in whatever game you choose.

Don't forget to let your child have a turn to be the leader, and see what sounds you recognize!

Music Drawing | 2 YEARS TO 12 YEARS

Listening to music while drawing can be a way to associate sounds with a pleasant activity. An art teacher taught me this when I was young, and I have since done this lovely activity with many children. It's a way of absorbing sound with your whole body and translating it into art.

To play this game, you just need a piece of paper—the larger the better—and a marker. While the music is playing, the "artist" just draws whatever lines they want. They could be wavy intersecting lines or straight connecting lines. It doesn't matter, and there are no mistakes. Anything drawn is just right.

When it feels right, change the music so that your artist (and you if you are joining in) can feel how the different music inspires you to create different lines, circles, and motion. It also helps the child with sound sensitivity enlarge their acceptance.

To complete the exercise, have a wide range of crayons or markers available so that each little section of the free-range drawing can be filled in with color. In the end you'll have a musical display and a work of art.

MODIFICATIONS FOR OLDER KIDS: Coloring books made for adults are all the rage these days. There are many different types available online or in bookstores, and they are quite intricate; they would be enjoyed by older children as well as adults.

Dancing Hands | 2 YEARS TO 12 YEARS

 There are quite a few games that can help your child develop an awareness of sound, and they only require each other's hands. Start off with Dancing Hands. You can hold hands or keep them separate. Put on some music, and make your hands move to the sounds. Classical music might invoke swaying hands, while calypso sounds get the fingers jumping. If you want to literally use just fingers, your pointer and middle fingers could dance on the table. Or maybe your hands would prefer to play air guitar or air piano. That's fine, too. The more variations in music you can find, the better.

If you don't have access to music or you want to go on to new games, let your hand hear the beat with Rhythmic Hands. Experiment with different rhythms. Maybe start with an old rhythm you might remember from your childhood called "Shave and Haircut—Two Bits." Or you might do a three-point rhythm with the emphasis on the first downbeat, or maybe the first beat is soft and the other two are louder.

If your inner drummer is not inspired, play Syllable Hands and use names and clap for each syllable. Oliver has three claps and Olivia has four. Clap out the beats in every family member's and friend's name, including, of course, the family dog and cat!

Even though this game is all about hands, it's really all about sounds. You're increasing your child's awareness of sounds; kids who seem to be oblivious will start to notice differences in sound. And those children who are supersensitive will find that they can tolerate a larger variation in sounds than they thought.

Getting Warmer | 2 YEARS TO 12 YEARS

Getting Warmer is a game that can be played spontaneously and be a fun response to everyday questions that you know the answers to, such as "Where's the glue?" or "Have you seen my doll?"

The boring answer would be "In the top drawer." The annoying answer would be "Right where you left it." The fun answer would be "Let's play Getting Warmer."

This is how it's done: Whenever your child is near the desired object, you say, "Getting warmer." When they move farther from the object, you say, "Getting colder." When they are very close to the object, you can elaborate and say, "You are getting so hot!" or "You are going to burn!" The opposite would be to elaborate by saying, "You are freezing!" "You are turning into ice!"

For the child who tends not to listen or doesn't listen well, there is an immediate reward for listening well—they get what they want!

You don't need to wait for a question to play this game, of course. You can hide treats, and the child has to find them by listening to your clues. Even opening birthday presents can be prolonged and made into an auditory experience if you play Getting Warmer for each gift.

Stick this game in whenever you want during the day. You might be surprised how well it's received even if it is played a lot.

Blind Walk to My Tree | 3 YEARS TO 7 YEARS

 Go outside with your child, and use a blindfold or a paper bag to block all their vision except their feet.

Starting at the house or edge of the yard, direct the child to a tree by giving verbal directions. "Go straight—stop. Turn to your right and walk five steps—stop. Now turn to your left and walk eight steps—stop." And so on until the child reaches a tree. Tell them to hug that tree. Then stop.

Now direct the child back, one verbal clue at a time, to the beginning spot.

The game then is to find that tree without the blindfold on. The child can try and hug different trees, but "their" tree will feel different: it was bigger than their hands could reach around, the bark felt very rough, if it had a smell, and so on.

The game is really all about listening to clues and following them so your child will be more attuned to his auditory sense. But if it means that your kid now has a special relationship with the tree of your choice, that's *amore*!

Red Light / Green Light | 3 YEARS TO 12 YEARS

Children with SPD sometimes have an on button, but not an off. They know how to go but are not necessarily so good with how to stop. It can make life scary for parents who see that their little one seems to lack the sense of danger and will run into the busy street or in the deep water without a hint of caution.

Red Light / Green Light gives children an opportunity to hear these words of caution, to have to respond to the words of exclamation—specifically, stop!

This game can be played when the child is on foot in the house or on a trike in the yard. Begin by announcing the game: "Let's play Red Light / Green Light. When I say 'green light,' run. When I say 'red light,' stop."

Stand in front of your child and say "green light" and move aside, letting them pass. Then, in a few seconds, say "red light!" You can step in front of the child, blocking their path if you need to.

Vary the speed of the light. Sometimes it stays green for a longer while, while other times it's very short. If you make the length vary, your child has to listen to know what to do. If your tone and intentions are playful, the child will get into the spirit of the game, even if they are slow to catch on.

Want to do this game in other ways or other places? Play the game in slow motion or on the beach in thick sand, where running is naturally slower. Or add visuals by making up a sign that says "stop" on one side and "go" on the other to accompany your verbal orders.

Birds Sing, Insects Hum | 3 YEARS TO 12 YEARS

Birdies sing first thing in the morning, when they are saying hello to the day, and again at dusk, when day is done. It's an ideal opportunity to sit outside and listen. When you listen, *really* listen, to the sounds, you can start to make out the different calls birds make. Although it is good information, you don't have to know which bird says what to make its song. In this game, it's more about imitating the bird sounds. It's also about locating sound, a problem some children have. Can you figure out where the sound is coming from and find the bird? Can you imitate the longer sounds the dove makes or the chirps of the canary? What are the distinctive sounds birds make in your part of the world?

If your child seems interested in expanding their auditory awareness and tolerance, you could get serious and get on the Web for more sounds and information.

Your child might be interested to know that birds use songs and calls to reinforce their territories, attract mates, identify one another, warn other birds about predators, and tell other birds about food. Calls are shorter than songs, and birdcalls can be a handy tool for finding and identifying different birds, if your child is interested.

Recordings are available if sitting outside isn't feasible. Websites such as that of the Cornell Lab of Ornithology have an online bird guide that contains a variety of different calls and songs. When children listen to recordings, they might also note the rhythm, pitch, tone, and repetition patterns of the calls and really enlarge their awareness of the nuances of sound.

Going on a bird-watching field trip with a local group can be a good addition to your child's life, and this way they can work on visual and social skills at the same time.

Your child may get so good at hearing different sounds that they start identifying the different hum of insects!

Play Your Own Sound | 5 YEARS TO 12 YEARS

Whether your child is oblivious to sound or has a small window of tolerated sounds, you can increase awareness and tolerance by letting them make their own music.

Which instrument is chosen depends, of course, on the interest of your child. For a very young one, a set of pots and pans and a wooden spoon are ideal. You can point out the difference in sound between the plastic bowl and the metal one. You can make simple rhythms for your young one to imitate, or better yet, imitate any rhythm the child comes up with.

For the older child, a trip to a music store or the musical section in the toy store might be in order. A slide whistle might be too shrill, but a kazoo, on which you hum your own sound, might be perfect. The kazoo might lead to a harmonica. A recorder might lead to a flute. Strumming a ukulele could start so simply but turn beautifully complex. And there's nothing wrong with a cheap electric guitar and amp.

Whether a simple instrument leads to a more complex one isn't the point of this activity, although it might be a benefit. It's more important that your child take control over the range of sounds that they hear by making their own.

You might want to do what I did and hire a teacher to come to the house and teach everyone to play together. We all learned to play "Amazing Grace." It wasn't at all graceful, but we did have some amazing moments when we were hearing each other and playing together.

Let's Tell Stories | 5 YEARS TO 12 YEARS

 This is my favorite listening game of all time, and I've played it a lot. In this game, two or more people tell a story. One person starts the story and just says a line or two or three, and then the other person has to pick up the story from there and add a little bit. Each person has to listen to what came before to advance the story.

It's an especially good game to play in the car, where you can keep your eyes on the road and still have a fun conversation with your child or children.

The first person starts off the story. I like to start with the words "Once upon a time" because it's so traditional and signals the other player that you are about to start this soon-to-be favorite game.

The best part of this game is that you as a parent know what interests your child, so you can make the characters be people in the family or people or things in their fantasy or TV world. Even an older child can play this game if you make the characters in the story people or things your child cares about.

What I especially like about this game is that the story doesn't even have to make sense. It's good if the last person leaves an opening line, such as "And then they went into the room and saw . . ."

But if the next person said "hippopotamus" and went on about hippos, even though the beginning of the story was about dragons, no problem. We call that "artist's license" because each player is free to be a creative artist and add to the story in their own manner.

Remember, this is also good for little ones who have less experience with stories but can use work on listening. Their story could be about the simple things in Big Bird's day or their own day, starting with waking up and eating breakfast.

The point is to listen to what others have said and go from there—or take it to a very different place.

This game can last a long time and is perfect to play on a road trip:

- "Once upon a time there was this mouse who liked to play with elephants. One day he saw an elephant, and he said . . ."

- "Will you play with me? But the elephant said, 'No!' And the donkey said, 'Why not?' And the elephant said . . ."

- "Because you are too little, and I only like to play with . . ."

- And so on and so on and so on.

Another variation to making up your own stories is to read the storybooks you have but change the name of the characters. The Berenstain Bears could be renamed as people in your own family!

MODIFICATIONS FOR OLDER KIDS: Raise the intrigue bar of storytelling. Try a story about teachers at school doing funny things that he wouldn't expect. Take it outside at dark and initiate a ghost story!

Water Glasses | 5 YEARS TO 12 YEARS

 Different levels of water in glasses make different sounds. You might have seen this done but never tried it. It's a wonderful listening game and fun to do. Set it up by taking a set of glasses and pouring different levels of water in each glass, starting with a small amount in the first glass and progressively more in the other glasses. Eight glasses should do nicely. If you don't have enough glasses, go to a secondhand store and buy a bunch. Or purchase a box of canning jars and use those. Once your glasses are set up, try these games:

- Tap each glass with a spoon, and listen to the different tones.

- Listen closely, and see if you both can imitate those individual sounds with your voice.

- Make two sets of glasses, and make your sounds match.

- See if you can play a specific simple tune, such as "Row, Row, Row Your Boat."

- Play around with the different sounds, and make your own tune.

- Make up words to go with your unique tune.

Just have fun making music with no goal in mind at all.

Games for Gross Motor Skills

Gross motor skills are those that involve the large muscles of the body. As opposed to fine motor skills, which use the small muscles of the fingers, toes, wrists, lips, and tongue, our gross motor skills are the bigger movements, which use the large muscles in the arms, legs, torso, and feet.

Because of gross motor skills, we can stand, walk, run, climb, skip, jump, throw a ball, and perform everyday functions. Gross motor skills impact more than just everyday movement; they influence children's academic learning by affecting their posture and ability to sit at a desk, and even by providing the strength and endurance they need to get through the school day. They are needed to do self-care when dressing and putting on pants, one leg at a time. Gross motor skills also affect core strength, which is needed for fine motor skills such as writing and cutting.

This is one of the few areas where hyper-responsiveness can actually be a good thing. Children with strong gross motor skills tend to be quite athletic. But conversely, there is both a physical and an emotional impact associated with poor—or hypo-responsive—gross motor skills. They affect children's self-esteem in sporting activities when they want to fit in and play the physical games that others do. Nobody wants to be picked last, and certainly nobody likes to be bullied—two damaging consequences that these children sometimes face.

Fortunately, gross motor skills can be learned. We can work on our gross motor skills by strengthening our core muscles and by learning to pay attention to our movements (proprioceptive) and balance (vestibular) senses, which tell us what our bodies are doing at every moment. We can learn to integrate our sensory systems to develop eye-hand coordination for better ball skills (throwing, catching, kicking) and general coordination when we integrate multiple movements.

We first start learning to use gross motor skills from birth, when we are born into a body we have no clue how to make work for us.

If your child has difficulties with gross motor skills, it is recommended you consult an occupational therapist. It may also be appropriate to consult a physiotherapist for gross motor skills. It is important to acknowledge, however, that in many pediatric cases, there is a large overlap in the skills addressed by physiotherapy and occupational therapy.

Look at newborns crying and flailing their limbs. But that same child will learn, experience by experience, how to differentiate their limbs so they can use them together or separately. The child learns how to strengthen core muscles to sit up, and learns how to work the side muscles to crawl and walk.

Supposedly, a child who doesn't go through the crawling stage will have problems with balance and coordinating both sides of their body, through the awareness gained from first lifting their head, then moving on all fours. I learned that although this is generally true, there are other ways to learn the same skills.

Many years ago I was in Bali, and there I learned that Hindus have a belief that babies are gods and should not touch the ground with their feet until a year old, when they have an official ceremony. Until then, babies are kept on their mothers' backs, and feel her walking rhythm and warmth. I was at a ceremony when a baby's feet first touched the ground and she took her own weight. I worried that later there would be a balance issue. But then I saw how toddlers practiced walking in sand (good balance work on uneven terrain) and carrying things on their head just like mom did (good postural work). I could see that there are other ways to work on these skills. It's never too late to work on skills, and there are multiple ways to do it.

GOALS OF THE GAMES

The games in this chapter use many methods to develop gross motor skills. You already know many games and hopefully take advantage of the local playground. I've added to your repertoire by purposely using easy-to-find material such as plastic bottles and rope, so practicing to improve your child's skills can be done easily at home. Find the games that are fun for you both, and enjoy the learning. We can help children improve their gross motor skills by:

- improving attention to task and alertness levels in readiness to respond quickly when they lose their balance, and to respond to changes in the environment around them;

- strengthening the body's core to provide greater body (especially trunk) stability;

- building general muscle strength where "floppy" muscles are a challenge;

- simplifying specific physical skills into one- or two-step components to teach the skill, then gradually add in components until the skill is able to be done in its entirety (e.g., skipping—start with a step, then a hop);

- gradually increasing duration and intensity of activity to increase endurance;

- improving sensory processing to ensure appropriate attention and arousal to attempt the tasks, as well as ensuring the body is receiving and interpreting the correct messages from the muscles in terms of their position, their relationship to one another, the speed at which they move, and how much force they are using;

- using cognitive planning strategies to talk the child through tasks; and

- utilizing a multisensory approach (using several of the seven senses) to learn new skills, which ensures a child has the best chance at learning appropriate strategies to respond to a physical challenge;

- developing skills necessary to support whole-body (gross motor) skills, including balance and coordination, strength and endurance, attention and alertness (sensory processing), body awareness, and movement planning (praxis).

Physical Activities to Help Improve Gross Motor Skills

1. **Hopscotch** for hopping
2. **Simon Says** for body awareness and movement planning
3. **Wheelbarrow walking races** for upper-body strength
4. **Walking on unstable surfaces** such as sand
5. **Climbing up and over objects,** such as large pillows or hills, to increase overall body strength
6. **Catching and balancing,** such as standing on one foot while catching a ball

Batting with Balloons | 1 YEAR TO 7 YEARS

Baseball and T-ball may be fun, but those balls can hurt and are hard to hit. And if you are a new learner who is just getting the sense of keeping your eye on the ball, they can be tough to get the hang of. For young ones just learning eye-hand coordination, use a balloon!

Make a bat out of anything handy, such as a paper towel tube or a rolled-up section of newspaper secured with tape. If you want a bat that will last, try using a large two-liter plastic bottle, the kind soft drinks come in. Cut a dowel or stick to fit inside the opening of the plastic bottle. Wrap some duct tape around the dowel and bottle opening to keep it secure, and voilà; you have a nifty bat.

Give the bat to your player, set them up in a good baseball stance, step back, and toss the balloon at them. The slow movement of a balloon floating toward the child gives them plenty of time to line up the bat, swing at the "ball," and get the satisfaction of "connecting."

If it is just the two of you, take turns being the pitcher/catcher and the batter. If there are other players, have them catch the "ball" as it leisurely floats down. Whoever catches it can be the batter next, though make sure everyone gets a turn eventually!

You could also hang the balloon from a low tree branch so that it's at the right height for your child to hit with a bat. The balloon or a regular ball can be put inside a torn pair of panty hose or a net bag and hung. Let your child whack away to their heart's content!

Want more balloon games? See how long you can keep the balloon in the air with everyone using their own soft bat, if your group is sufficiently coordinated not to bop one another on the head. If you don't have enough bats made, use flyswatters, Ping-Pong paddles, or tennis rackets.

You could both lie on the floor and keep the balloon in the air—try it with feet only. Tie a length of string to the balloon and then around your child's wrist. See how many times they can hit the balloon without missing.

Rope Games | 1 YEAR TO 10 YEARS

Ropes are wonderful for increasing gross motor skills. Jumping rope by yourself or playing double Dutch with other children in the playground can provide fun and excellent practice in developing skills.

This series of games involves jumping, leaping, and crawling, and it's easy to do at home.

For the child who is hesitant to jump or leap, try using the "voice-over" technique, where you act as if they are in the Olympics doing amazing feats: "And now Melanie will do a stupendous leap as she runs and jumps over the rope! One, two, three—there she goes. It's a winning leap! The crowd goes wild!"

FIRST YOU JUMP

Start the rope low, maybe even lying directly on the ground. Have the child stand in front of the rope and jump over, landing on both feet. Then, after each successful turn, raise the rope a little higher. You want to make the game within the child's abilities; they must feel confident to jump. As the game progresses, you can raise it slightly higher to increase the challenge.

Jumping over forward is one game. After the rope is as high as it should safely go, change the game by asking your child to jump different ways. "Can you jump over it while standing sideways to the rope? Can you jump over it while standing backward? How about hopping on one foot over the rope?"

THEN YOU LEAP

In this variation of the rope game, the player stands a distance from the rope, say about five feet, then runs and leaps over the rope, one foot leading. Instead of both feet hitting the floor or yard at the same time, one foot lands first and the other foot follows. Again you could put a small mat down a distance from the rope so she knows where to start the run.

If you add a "drumroll" to this leaping game, it adds to the excitement. You can do it with sound, such as one sound when running and a different, louder sound when leaping. "*Da-da-da-da-da* boom!*" Just be sure to hold the rope very loosely so your child doesn't trip, and if the rope is hit, it will just fall to the ground. Crêpe paper or streamers are good alternatives that won't trip up a child—it will just tear like the finish line at a race.

Recognizing how much energy it takes to jump over an increasingly higher rope encourages awareness of the proprioceptive sense. Feeling the difference between jumping over a rope from a standing position and leaping over the rope after running stimulates an awareness of how to move one's body in different ways. Use both methods to increase body awareness and motor skills.

If you don't have a rope, you can use scarves, ribbons, or even tube socks tied together. If there aren't two people to hold the ends, tie one end to a table leg or something stable, and that will work fine.

LAST, YOU CROUCH AND CRAWL

If you want another variation, start the rope at a height that requires your child to bend their head to go under. You keep lowering the rope on each round until your child needs to do a belly crawl to go under it.

Ask the child to go under the rope without touching it with any part of their body. I like to pretend that the rope is sizzling hot. Touch it, make a sizzle sound, and pull your hand away quickly, as if the rope is too hot to touch. Ask your child—for their own "protection"—to not touch the rope with any body part. Even while the child is going under the rope, say "Be careful!" The "hot" rope reminds your child to stay low.

Keep lowering the rope so your child has to adjust her body to fit under it without touching. When children have to keep lowering their bodies to go under a rope that keeps lowering, they become more aware of body movement and how much space their body takes up.

You can get a lot of mileage gaining gross motor skills with just a piece of rope.

Running Fast | 2 YEARS TO 5 YEARS

If I want to give a child a thrill, I get another adult, put the child in between us, take her hands, and run! And not just a jog or a pleasant run—I'm talking a full-on run. The point is to run faster than they can run by themselves. Kids giggle, and sometimes we have to help them not fall, but they want to do it again and again. It's a lot of fun to go faster than your legs will take you.

I keep the anticipation high by preparing for the run. I might use the old "One, two, three, go!" or "Ready, set, go!" Or I may make a motor sound such as *ru-ru-ru-ru-ru-run* to give them the sense that something exciting is going to happen.

MODIFICATIONS FOR OLDER KIDS: If your child already runs faster than you can run, you'll have to change the game. You can turn a running-fast game into a race. Adding elements to the race encourages a child to not just go wild, but to also go wild with awareness. Maybe the two of you, or your child and a playmate, have to race to the tree and back, but when they get to the tree, they have to go around it three times, and when they run back, they have to run back backward. If you don't want to race with them, you can be the person leisurely sitting in a chair in the shade with a stopwatch. "Ready, set, go! You did it in 180 seconds! Can you do it faster?"

Jumping, Hopping, and Skipping | 2 YEARS TO 10 YEARS

One hesitates to say something such as "All children with sensory problems like to jump." But I find this to be true more often than not. If I meet a young child comes who is either very shy or very boisterous, two opposite attitudes, I am surprised how often they will let me pick them up—even if very slightly—and jump them. I know that children on the sensory spectrum very often like deep proprioceptive stimulation, and nothing says proprioception like a good jump.

It's so easy to get a jumping game going. If you're outside, all you need is chalk or rocks as marking tools. If you're inside, all you need are sections of newspaper. If you're at a birthday party or it's Christmas, wrapping paper torn into small pieces works fine, too.

Place the markers or chalk marks at varying distances from one another. When they are placed near one another, the children take small jumps. When they are placed a greater distance from one another, the children need to do a larger jump. But best is that some are close together and some far apart, so children use their eyes and their eye-foot coordination to aim for the next spot, no matter how close or far away.

Know your child's abilities, or start with the easiest variation and lay the markers in a row about a foot apart (or whatever distance is appropriately easy). The object of the game is for the players to jump from the first paper, then to the second, third, and so on.

This is a gross motor learning game because in order to jump, children need to learn how to use the bottom half of their bodies independently from the top half. The top half stays relaxed, and the bottom half bends and pushes up. (When you see a toddler imitating a jump by using their arms and legs but not catching much air, the child is almost there).

Separating the top half of the body from the bottom is a development skill. The next development stage is separating one side of the body from the other. So if your child is ready for this stage, ask him to hop from marker to marker on one foot, then on the other.

Once kids can jump and then hop, the last stage is skipping. If your child is ready to skip, which is hopping rhythmically from one side to the other, you can hold hands and skip off into the sunset together. And if you've ever skipped with someone, you know *that* is fun!

MODIFICATIONS FOR OLDER KIDS: Older kids are likely to accept the challenge of jumping from here to there or show how high they can jump in place. You can encourage that by having them jump up beside a wall and mark with a Post-it how high they can touch on the wall. Jump many times, and see how high they can get the Post-its.

Obstacle Course | 2 YEARS TO 12 YEARS

 An obstacle course is a fun thing to construct out of household furniture. This will give your child a chance to practice motor skills by going over, under, and around obstacles. When constructing a course in your living room, think about these features:

- **Think prepositions.** Something to go *under, over, around, between,* and *across.*

- **Think directionally.** Something to climb *up, down, into,* and *out of.*

- **Think action verbs.** Something to *jump* over; *climb* on; *skip* around; *walk* forward, backward, or sideways to; *crawl* to or under; and *run* to.

Mark the start of the obstacle course with a piece of paper or rug or anything that defines that space as the beginning.

You could start with a chair to climb up on and jump off of or go under a table and go around the sofa. Perhaps jump over some cushions and get inside of the legs of an upside-down chair. There could be kitchen chairs placed back-to-back to go through, or a series of different-sized books, including a large hardcover to step over. Overturned chairs make a good tunnel for crawling through.

Look around the house, and add pieces, such as stools to jump from and large books to jump over.

Consider your child's level. How big of a jump is appropriate? Too high, they'll fall. Too low, it won't be challenging.

If you are outdoors, you can go nuts using whatever you want. Use hula-hoops, pool noodles, cones, ladders, tires, rope, and buckets. Just follow the same preposition rules—over, under, around, through, and so on.

You can let your child move things around and come up with her own obstacle course. The same material in a different order is an entirely different course!

Here are some items you could use:

- a fallen log to cross over
- a tree to skip around
- a branch to swing from
- a rock to climb up and jump off
- sidewalk squares to jump on, from one to another
- a street lamp to run to, touch, and run back from

Add a stopwatch, and see how fast your child can do the course. If you want more variation, have the child to do the whole course like a soldier, belly-down, pulling forward with elbows. Talk about a workout!

And if you want your child to go through a mud puddle as part of the course, that's up to the two of you. However, you might want to add a run through the sprinkler at the end!

Hula-Hoop Games | 2 YEARS TO 12 YEARS

 Hula-hoops, a long-ago fad, are usually twirled around the waist, gyrating the hips and using a rhythmic knee action to keep the hoop going. But there is so much more to do with hoops and a lot of skills to learn from using them. Get five or six of them from a dollar store and try these variations:

- **Jumping:** Lay them out in a straight line, and have your child jump from the first to the last. If this is successful, increase the difficulty by having the child jump to every other hoop or jump them while going backward or sideways. This game also works on stimulating the proprioceptive system and can thrill sensory seekers.

- **Patterns:** Instead of laying them out in a line, lay them out in a hopscotch pattern or in no particular pattern at all. Have your child decide what is done in each hoop. Maybe they jump in the first, squat and touch the ground in the second, do a spin in the third, and so on. This game also hones creativity and memory skills.

- **Overlapping:** Lay them out in a line, but overlapping one another. When a player goes from one end of the line to the other end, the goal is to tiptoe, making sure to step only in the empty spaces. You can pretend the hoops are electrified, and that they better be careful not to step on a hoop—only in the spaces in between!

This game also works on balance because tiptoeing is required.

- **Off the floor:** If you have another adult, you can both use the preceding pattern, but hold each hoop up so they're about six inches off the floor. Now it's trickier to put your feet into the empty spaces, as you have to lift your leg up to climb over the hoop into the next space. This game also works on motor planning, or knowing how to move your body to accomplish the task.

- **Tunnel:** Hold the hoops sideways so they form a tunnel. Again, another adult or older child is helpful if you want to make the tunnel longer. The children have to bend down to go under the hoops and all the way through the tunnel. If you have the hoops held at different heights, some higher than others, they have to adjust their body to go through without touching the hoops. This game also works on body awareness and how much space your body takes up.

- **Tunnel jump:** Hold up one or two hoops to form a tunnel, but have a huge pillow or mat on the other end. Children throw themselves through the hoop like a circus tiger and onto the mat. If they want to get fancy, they can do a somersault or Olympic-style landing when they get to the mat. This game stimulates the movement and balance senses.

- **Jump rope:** Have your child start with the hoop behind them while holding onto the sides. Then, instruct your child to bring the hoop up and around, and when it gets to the feet, jump over it. Repeat, repeat, repeat. The challenge: How many jumps are possible in a minute?

- **Roll:** Holding the hoop on its side with one hand, push the hoop forward with the other. If done correctly, it should smoothly roll from one person to another. Sometimes it will wobble as it rolls, but keep practicing and it works well. Take a step back each round to increase the distance—see how far you can go. This game also works on bilateral skills, where one hand does one thing and the other hand does another.

- **Kick:** If you've mastered the roll as previously described, the receiving person kicks the hoop as it comes to them. If kicked with the side of the foot, it will bounce high in the air and the other person can catch it. This game also works on balance and timing.

- **Toss:** If you put an object such as a cone or block of wood on the ground, your player can hold the hoop by its side and toss it over the object. If you're feeling brave and trusting, you could be the object and your child tosses the hoop over you. This game works on eye-hand coordination.

You and your child might come up with 10 more games to play with hoops!

Plastic Bottle Games | 3 YEARS TO 12 YEARS

 Like it or not, plastic water bottles are part of our lives.

Until that time when plastic bottles are eliminated, we can do our part in reusing them by making games that will help our children learn to coordinate their muscles.

Children can bowl them down and leap over them to have fun and learn ways to use their bodies to do what they want. Knowing which muscles to use to throw a ball accurately requires body awareness. Knowing how far and high to jump to go over obstacles also takes knowing which muscles to use to accomplish the task.

BOWL

You can set up a bunch of bottles into a traditional pyramid triangle such as in a bowling alley, either on a table or on the ground. Using a light ball, a beach ball, or a soft rubber ball, see how many you can knock down in one throw (or roll) or in several throws. Keep throwing until no bottle is left standing.

Instead of a pyramid, place the bottles in one long row facing the thrower. How far apart to place the bottles depends upon how challenging you want the game to be. The closer the bottles are to one another, the easier they are to knock down. If you want to make the bottles harder to knock over, fill them with water or sand first. If you want to get fancy, get the children involved by adding color. Before they even begin to play, they can add food dye to the water in the bottles. This could be a teachable moment in which they learn that, for example, a drop of red food coloring and a drop of yellow make orange-colored water. If you do add water, tighten the caps well or wrap with tape to prevent possible leaking when they are knocked down.

The size of the ball can vary. You could use anything from a tennis ball size to soccer ball size in the same game. Start with the larger size. Remember, when using a smaller-sized ball, it is a bit easier if the bottles are closer together.

If you want to add an academic skill to this game, ask your player how many bottles were knocked down each time.

If you want to add the element of surprise, you can add water to the beach ball when you blow it up. The water makes the movement of the ball unpredictable, and that can add to the fun of the game.

LEAP

This is a progressive game in which you start by placing one bottle in front of your child with the challenge, "Can you jump over this?"

Whether the bottle is standing upright or lying on its side depends on your child's skill. If you aren't sure, always start with what's easiest. After the child jumps over the one bottle and shows you that it was "easy peasy lemon squeezy," you up the challenge and add another bottle.

"Can you jump over both of these?"

To make it more challenging, add variations such as jumping over them backward, sideways, or on one foot. Then, let your child direct and challenge you. How many bottles can you jump over: Four? Five? Find out!

TOSS

There is still something else you can do with these bottles, and that is to toss them around.

Have your player experiment with the following variations:

- Toss the bottle from one hand to the other.
- Toss the bottle in the air with both hands and catch— toss the bottle in the air.
- Toss it in the air, clap once, then catch. Add a second clap, then a third, and so on.
- Toss it up and catch with the dominant hand.
- Toss it up and catch with the nondominant hand.
- Toss it up and make it twirl before catching it.
- Toss it to another person.

If you play the game with your child, every time the other person catches the bottle, take a step away from each other, making the distance between you longer. Every time the other person *doesn't* catch the bottle, take a step toward each other, making the distance between you shorter.

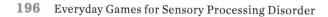

Animal Walks | 3 YEARS TO 12 YEARS

Animals walk in different ways. A crab has its own way of moving—scuttling—which is very different from the horse and the kangaroo. Asking children to imitate the ways different animals move is an excellent way for them to become aware of their bodies and how to move them in various ways.

Besides working on gross motor skills requiring core strength and balance, this job of being an animal is a form of "heavy work" because all the muscles are being used. This can be calming for a child who is a sensory seeker.

In this game, your participation is key because you both may need to figure out how to do these different movements together. Want to add sound to the movements? Hmm, what does a crab say, anyway?

Here are some to start with:

- **Kangaroo:** Hold hands bent at chest and hanging limply. Put feet together, bend knees, and jump forward.

- **Crab:** Squat and reach backward with arms, hands flat on floor. Keeping head up, bottom near the floor, and knees bent, scuttle across the floor, keeping this position.

- **Penguin:** Waddle from side to side on your heels with your arms by your sides.

- **Seal:** Lie on the floor, belly down. Push up the body by extending the arms straight down. Walk forward with your hands, and drag your feet behind.

- **Tiger:** Crouch on all fours with hands in claw position. Lift rear end to scout for prey, and then get up on knees from crawling to roar!

- **Crocodile:** Lay on your belly with arms and legs bent. Move the right side, arm, and leg together, and then the left side together.

- **Frog:** Squat low and place hands on the floor in front of you. Move the hands forward. Then bring the feet forward in a little jump.

- **Horse:** Gallop and whinny while you run around. Buck your head up and down. Lift your knees high, and point your toes like a prancing horse.

- **Monkey:** Run around with knees slightly bent and both hands grazing the floor. Don't forget to scratch your sides and pick "bugs" from your little one's hair!

- **Elephant:** Sway from side to side as you walk forward. Bend at the hips, and allow your arms to be loose except when one arm turns into the trunk and rises high!

- **Worm:** Raise body from lying position by putting arms and feet on the floor, supporting the body. Move the back feet toward your hands. Then move the hand forward. Keep moving forward inch by inch—it's slow going, but you're a worm! Move the other variations to Animal Walk include figuring out how animals might move, even animals you might not have seen move, such as an ostrich, a flamingo, or a scorpion.

You don't have to limit yourself to animals. You can both be a tornado, hurricane gales, or giant ocean waves, moving together!

Target Throws |

 Children who use too much force and inadvertently break pencil points or tear paper when erasing often need to learn how to control the force of their muscles to achieve different results.

In this game, they need to use good muscle strength to throw a long distance, but not as much to throw a smaller distance. This awareness of how much force is appropriate to accomplish a task is useful in many of life's scenarios. Beside pencil points, we need to know much force is needed to pat someone on the back so it doesn't hurt them.

To play this game, you need spears, but not the caveman kind with the pointy stone tip. Use the homemade kind that you can make out of newspaper or magazines.

If you roll up a newspaper, you have a long spear or javelin for longer distances and outdoor fun. A spear can also be made from a rolled-up page of a magazine and is better for inside the home and shorter throws.

The spears are then thrown at various targets.

Always begin at the child's skill level so they can start with success, and then suggest smaller and smaller objects to aim at. The easiest targets to begin with are a door, large chair, refrigerator, or any large unbreakable object.

You can make those same large objects harder by drawing a target on them. A refrigerator is easy to hit, but a large circle taped on the refrigerator is a bit harder. A smaller and smaller circle increases the challenge.

You can add academic variations: "Throw this at something that is red [or round or fuzzy or starts with the letter *B*]."

If you don't mind preparing in advance, hang pieces of colored construction from clothesline (or evenly spaced pair of trees, posts, or anything from which you can string a line), and have your player aim at the colors you name or just at any paper. Older kids can make up their own targets—objects that are smaller and farther away require more-mature throwing skills.

You can also use balls and provide indoor targets such as a wastebasket, a dishpan, buckets, boxes, and shoes. Give a point score to each target, but make the scoring humorous. For example, the wastebasket could be worth a zillion points and the dishpan a gazillion points! Outdoor targets could be an inner tube, a bicycle tire, a coiled garden hose, street signs, a hole in the ground, big rocks, and telephone poles.

Take turns with this game, and if possible, include siblings and others, too. Throwing and aiming require eye-hand coordination skills that all children enjoy.

Toe Stepping | 5 YEARS TO 12 YEARS

 This is a fun and silly game that requires concentration and quick movement.

Two people, both barefoot or in socks, face each other and hold hands. Each person tries to step on the other's toes while at the same time keeping their toes from being stepped on.

You might remind your partner that players are to step lightly on each other's toes. The golden rule: "Step on others as you would want to be stepped on!"

Learning to concentrate on keeping out of the way while going for the goal is a kind of trial by fire. Pressure on their foot lets them know when they weren't quick enough to get out of the way!

Games for Fine Motor Skills

Motor skills are actions that involve the movement of muscles in the body. They are divided into two groups: fine motor skills and gross motor skills. Fine motor refers to the small movements of the hands, wrists, fingers, feet, toes, lips, and tongue. We couldn't tie our shoes, lick an ice cream cone, or grasp an object between the thumb and a finger without the help of our fine motor skills.

Gross motor skills include the larger movements of arms, legs, feet, or the entire body and are responsible for our ability to crawl, run, jump, and skip.

Both types of motor skills usually develop together, because many activities depend on the coordination of gross and fine motor skills.

For fine motor mastery, we especially need to develop control of our hands, as we use them to help with all our daily activities, such as eating, drinking, dressing ourselves, playing with objects, drawing, writing, holding small items, buttoning clothing, turning pages, eating, cutting with scissors, and using computer keyboards.

Fine motor skills require precision and coordination. Our hands are an intricate system of bones, nerves, and muscles that help us manipulate and explore objects. Learning to control the whole hand and each finger takes experience, and is precisely sequenced from the baby's first swatting hand motion, to the toddler's precise pincer grasp, to the student's perfect tripod writing grasp. As we develop, we become more and more dexterous and precise with our hands.

Our oral motor skills with our lips and tongue are similar, and their development follows a sequence. Each of our experiences, starting from nursing on the nipple to sucking on a straw, lays a foundation for the next skill.

Children with fine motor difficulties may demonstrate the following behaviors and characteristics:

- poor prewriting, drawing, and writing skills
- illegible handwriting
- difficulty using scissors, crayons, or silverware
- difficulty or inability to button, snap, zip, or fasten clothes
- awkwardness trying to string beads
- inconsistent use of their dominant hand
- poor strength and control in the hands
- poor coordination when using both hands together

- avoidance of fine motor tasks
- oral motor weakness

GOALS OF THE GAMES

We help children develop fine motor skills through practice, practice, and more practice. The games in this chapter help children who are having difficulty in this area get more practice learning to control their muscles in a fun and original way. The games encourage using, for example, items found in the kitchen to make art, or the dining table for a coin-flicking game, as ways to develop finger dexterity.

Fine motor development can also be encouraged by other activities that youngsters enjoy, including crafts, puzzles, building blocks, finger paints, Legos, tracing letters, and even popping bubbles on bubble wrap with just the index finger and thumb. Helping parents with everyday domestic activities, such as baking, can be fun for the child and help develop fine motor skills.

Water Bottle Drop | 1 YEAR TO 5 YEARS

 This simple fine motor game is an excellent way to improve finger dexterity and eye-hand coordination, and increase attention span. Cut up a straw into four or five pieces. Use about four straws, and put all the pieces in a pile. Use an empty plastic water bottle with the cap removed, and show your child how to put the straw pieces in the opening. The goal is to put each straw piece, one by one, into the opening. Once all the straw pieces are in the bottle, they can be poured out and the child can redo the game.

If you want to increase the challenge, use toothpicks. To make it even more challenging, keep the cap on the bottle and poke a hole in the cap about the size of a toothpick. If you don't have straws or toothpicks, you could use a pile of dried beans—lima beans are a good size—and have your child put these, one by one, into the bottle opening. No beans around? Try cut-up spaghetti!

MODIFICATIONS FOR OLDER KIDS: Vary the method used to get the items from the pile into the bottle. How about pinching the items between other fingers? Pinky and ring finger? The thumbs from each hand? Can the child pick the straw pieces up with chopsticks or two pencils and get them in the bottle? Play the game three times—and using a stopwatch, time the child and show them their progress.

Straw Worm | 1 YEAR TO 7 YEARS

 You can turn a straw wrapper into a surprising "live" creature and at the same time help a child stay focused and entertained while sitting at a restaurant. That your child is also getting an opportunity to practice fine motor control is icing on the cake.

Get a straw, and instead of pulling off the paper cover, squish it off so that it forms accordion pleats. Then place the straw into a glass of water. Put your finger on the top of the straw so it traps a little water in it. Hold the straw over the squished straw wrapper, and pick your finger up so a few drops fall on the wrapper. The wrapper will almost magically move like a wiggly worm. After you have demonstrated, let the child try. Your child will discover by experimenting that a little water makes the worm move, and too much water drowns it. This discovery will increase awareness of how much water becomes trapped in the straw, and what to do to get more or less water in the straw.

If you start to feel guilty because your child is overly enthusiastic about this game and using too many of the restaurant's straws, change the activity. See if your child can take water from one glass and fill up another using that newly learned straw-filling skill. And toss those extra straws in your purse to bring home for other fine motor games.

Clothespins on the Can | 2 YEARS TO 10 YEARS

 Sometimes the problem a child has with using their hands isn't lack of dexterity; it's lack of strength. This game addresses that issue with nothing more than clothespins and a can.

Take some clothespins and a large can, such as the kind coffee or peaches come in, and clip the clothespins all around the rim. The game is to pull all the clothespins off, then put them back on again.

You would think children would see this activity as going nowhere—clothespins off, clothespins on—but that's because we adults are stuck on the results. Little ones still love the process—I've seen many children fascinated with this task.

The clothespins that have springs in them are usually used. But if you have the old-fashioned kind that just have a slit in them, those also add visual practice because they require some eye-hand coordination.

If you want to make this game double its fine motor purpose, have the child paint faces on the wooden clothespins with paint or markers first. If you paint the clothespin a solid color, you can talk about colors: "Put on the red ones first," for example. If you paint faces on the clothespins, you can name the characters and encourage fantasy and creativity as they are posed at the top of their can castle.

If you want to change the game entirely, put a crayon in the clothespin, and then put the crayon/clothespin between your big and second toes. See if you can draw a line, shape, or letter on a piece of paper.

Art for Two | 2 YEARS TO 10 YEARS

If you've got a little money, you can never go wrong buying your child a ream of paper and Magic Markers to make visual arts (simultaneously working those fine motor skills!) wherever the mood strikes. Even the most resistant writer will be pleased if you pull these out during a long wait at the doctor's office.

With these supplies, you are ready for a great game of Art for Two. The way it starts off is to make a mark. It can be anything from a circle to a line. Just one mark. Your child then adds to your mark. Say you did a circle; your child might put spokes on your circle. Then it's your turn, and you add, say, little circles to the top of each spoke, and then pass it back. Keep switching colors so the drawing is colorful. You continue this way, back and forth, until you are both satisfied that the drawing is done. Both of your marks can be straight lines, wavy lines, circles, zigzags, anything! The only rule is that every person's mark must connect to the design that is already there.

As you know, the design is not the point. The point is to encourage your child to hold a pen and draw. If possible, encourage a three-point grasp. A three-point grasp, also called a tripod grasp, is the typical way adults hold a pen. Very young children, or those without good motor control, hold the pen in a whole-hand grasp. As they get older or learn more control, you can encourage, through demonstration and a few verbal cues, how to hold the pen with three fingers.

Bear in mind that a child who learns four elementary shapes can write every letter in the alphabet. These elementary shapes are the horizontal line, the vertical line, the diagonal line, and the circle.

Try it out yourself. Any letter in the alphabet has one or more of these shapes. A *K* is a vertical line and two diagonals. A *D* is a vertical line and half a circle. Knowing this simple fact can help children not be intimidated by the idea of writing letters. Start them off with the first letter of their name!

Kitchen Art | 2 YEARS TO 12 YEARS

The importance of the player to pay attention to what their fingers are doing is a large aspect of fine motor games. It turns out that the kitchen has many materials that will do just that, and make some art at the same time.

TOOTHPICK ART

Picking up small toothpicks may be a good fine motor skill, but putting them together takes a vision and brings it to the next level.

You can make specific things, such as shapes, squares, rectangles, or triangle. Letters that work particularly well with straight lines, such as *E* and *F* and *M*, are good, too. Then your child can imitate what you made. You could make the letters in their name and the names of family members. Then you can take a turn imitating what your child makes!

A very young child might appreciate your making a birthday cake out of play dough. First round, you put the toothpicks in the cake and sing. Then, on the second round, pull out the toothpicks, and then have the child re-insert the picks in the holes you made. This is a great way to develop eye-hand coordination.

CEREAL NECKLACE

Art can be beautiful, and art can be functional, but isn't it nice when it is also edible? And isn't it even better that the making of this lovely necklace is just right for developing fine motor control?

Give your child a piece of yarn, string, or dental tape, and the kind of cereal that has holes in the middle, such as Cheerios or Froot Loops.

Encourage your child to put the cereal pieces on the string. If you use yarn or string, it can be helpful to young ones to wrap a piece of tape on the stringing end so it's firmer and goes more easily through the hole in the cereal. Tie a fat knot at the other end so the cereal doesn't slip off. Give whatever assistance is needed to be successful. In the beginning you might need to hold the string steady.

When the child finishes, tie the ends of the yarn together to make a necklace. Have your child count how many pieces of cereal are on the string. Afterward, let your child eat a few pieces, and then count how many pieces are left—you might as well throw in some math for early learners!

If you want your necklace to be lasting, instead of edible, string other things, such as buttons, short pieces of colored straws, macaroni, or other hollow pasta shapes. Pretzels can be used for stringing, too, and the hole is bigger!

Instead of string or yarn, you could use pipe cleaners and turn the project into bracelets, rings for the fingers, or loops to hang around the ears. If you don't have cereal, use paper clips and have your child hook the paper clips into a chain necklace.

TURKEY BASTER ART

Put a little oil into a jar of water that has been colored with food coloring. Your child sucks up the concoction with the turkey baster and releases it on a piece of paper tucked in a baking sheet to contain the mess. Then spread the puddles of water out in an artistic way by blowing on them with a straw. It's true that one can't control the results when you're blowing with a straw. But with enough practice, you can strongly influence the art outcome!

FOOD SCULPTURES

Use toothpicks, uncooked fettuccine, or pretzel sticks, along with your choice of connectors, such as raisins, mini-marshmallows, or gumdrops. See if they can make an animal with these pieces, or an abstract design.

POTATO PEELER ART

Peeling anything is great for developing fine motor skills and strength. Apples, potatoes, carrots, chalk. *Chalk?* Yes! Use a potato peeler to scrape chalk into a bowl of water to create unique art. Your child can use different-colored chalk and keep scraping until a layer covers the top of the water. Then gently lay a piece of paper on top of the chalk pieces and let it soak in. The results may surprise you both once the paper dries; in fact, you might want to use this as wrapping paper for your next gift.

Practicing with Scissors | 3 YEARS TO 7 YEARS

When I ask parents if their preschool child knows how to use a pair of scissors, I often hear fears or actual tales of things like hair and bedcovers being cut. I, too, have such a story: My daughter once decided to cut her bangs. She cut them very, very short. When I looked aghast, she reassured me that if she just kept her eyebrows continually raised, her bangs would look the right length!

If your child can be trusted with scissors or you can provide supervision, there is an order to learning how to use this tool:

1. **Snip.** Cut a small strip of paper, and let your learner snip off small pieces.

2. **Cut on a line.** Use a piece that's a little larger and draw a line from one end to the other. Encourage your child to cut right on top of the line.

3. **Cut on a curved line.** Draw a curved line on the paper, and have your child follow the line when cutting.

4. **Cut on a zigzag line.** This kind of line requires stopping and starting, and turning the paper with the other hand.

5. **Cut a circle.** Again, this task requires good focusing and using the other hand to help guide the work.

Easy Hammering | 3 YEARS TO 10 YEARS

Hitting a nail with a hammer can be difficult. If you don't hit the nail just right, it is likely to bend, and hammering a bent nail is useless.

Yet hammering is still a good fine motor skill to teach and to learn, and a useful way to combine the visual and the motor sense. What I have done over the years is give children this experience by getting some foam blocks and golf tees. The foam provides just the right amount of resistance to hold a golf tee upright. When your child hits the golf tee with a tack hammer, it sinks nicely into the foam. You can substitute floral foam if you've got some. You could also use a toy or plastic hammer. Or, if you don't have a small-size hammer, you can use a rock. The beginner only has to hammer lightly to see results.

For a young child, start the game by pressing in the tips of golf tees or nails so that the head and most of its length protrude. Place the tees two to three inches apart. Demonstrate how to hammer the tees into the block. Then demonstrate how to pull the hammered tees back out of the foam using the claw end of the hammer. Then, let your child try, using a different area of the block and hammer again. If your child needs some help, you can prepare the foam block ahead of time by putting the tees/nails in the block and then pulling them out. This way, your child already has holes to make the hammering even easier. Putting the tees into the ready-made holes also develops good motor control.

Because hammering into foam is such a novel experience, it can capture the interest of a child who might otherwise be reluctant to do hand activities. The right-size foam is usually used for packing equipment, so if you don't have any handy, you can usually get some at an electronic store. Golf tees can be found at any store that sells sports equipment, but if you don't have golf tees, regular nails work, too. Ask for roofing nails because they have a flat, round head.

Recently I've noticed there is a commercial toy on the market that uses this exact same idea. Since I've been doing this idea for over 10 years, they might have gotten the idea from me (grin). Maybe not and it's just that good minds think alike. The commercial toy costs about $30, and it is a nice toy. Otherwise, to make your own, the golf tees cost about two dollars, and the foam and rock are free.

Pebblemania | 3 YEARS TO 10 YEARS

Little rocks, pebbles, and even gravel can have artistic uses and are super for helping develop fine motor control. Handling them to make a design enhances the use of the small muscles in the hand. If you don't have small rocks nearby, you can buy the glass kind sold in craft shops and dollar stores.

Put them in a large pile or bowl, and, one by one, let your child pick them up to make different shapes:

- one large square
- two small circles
- two intersecting circles
- a triangle
- two intersecting triangles, forming a star
- the child's name
- a body with arms and legs
- a road for a truck
- any design the child wants!

If each of you makes your own designs, you both reap the reward of focused tranquility by working quietly beside each other.

If you want the creation to last and if the stones are small enough, use white glue and attach the rocks to a piece of cardboard. The cardboard from cracker boxes is perfect. Or, take a photo with your phone, and show it to your artist. It's fun to see one's creations immortalized!

If your child starts to get bored with making all these designs, change the game. Get a wastebasket and ask your artist to throw the stones into it, one by one, with their toes.

Air-Dry Clay | 3 YEARS TO 10 YEARS

Playing with play dough or clay is always a good activity for little fingers. It develops both strength and dexterity.

Fairly new on the market is air-dry clay. It's a kind of clay that will harden when left overnight. No more need for baking in a toaster oven or a ceramic kiln. The advantage is that older children will enjoy using clay when they are too old for play dough. And children of all ages will be glad to see their project become permanent, and, if they want, they can paint it the next day.

If you need some ideas on how to get your youngster interested in clay, here are some beginning projects:

- **Make a ball.** The smaller the ball, the more control is required. You can start just squishing one together using your whole hand. But later, have your child work toward rolling one in the palms of their hands.

- **Roll a snake.** Roll a handful of clay back and forth on a table until it forms a snake. The more you roll it, the longer the snake gets. Add features to the snake. Little balls of clay can make the eyes. A slit on the end can be the mouth.

- **Build a snowman.** Three balls of different sizes make a snowperson, but your child can develop more fine motor control by making and adding tiny noses, hats, and scarves!

- **Make a birthday cake.** Any big lump of shaped clay can be a birthday cake. All you need to do is have your learner add some toothpicks for candles and pretend to light them. Time to sing the birthday song! You can give your child a butter or plastic knife to cut up and serve the cake so everyone can celebrate the birthday or un-birthday child!

Coin Play | 3 YEARS TO 12 YEARS

You always have some coins, and they are especially good for this fine motor game. You can play it at home or even at a restaurant when you're waiting for your food. There are many variations, so choose the one that is just right for you and your child. If there are a few people at the table, everyone can play. Give each player at the table a penny with the flat side on the table.

Move the penny along the table by flicking it with your index finger and thumb, or pushing it with just an index finger or the side of the thumb. The method doesn't matter. Here are some games:

- **Collision Course:** Partners sitting across from each other flick their pennies toward each other. One goal is to see if they can get their pennies to meet and collide in the middle. Another is to see who can get their penny closer to the other person without it sliding off the table.

- **Collision Course Plus:** If more than two want to play, have all the players flick their pennies into the center of the table and try to get the pennies to bump into each other or hit a specified object, such as the saltshaker. Whoever succeeds, or whoever comes closest, wins that round.

- **Goal Posts:** Set up two objects, such as two cups or just two other pennies, a short distance away from the players as "goal posts." The players have to flick their pennies between the two objects. Keep bringing the goal posts closer together to increase the challenge.

- **Coin Circle:** Put a bunch of coins in a circle and flick the coin at the circle. Whichever coins get moved, the flicker gets to keep.

- **Penny Line:** Make a line of pennies with at least an inch of space between them, and have a player try to flick a penny through each of the spaces. Or have the player try to hit each penny and knock it out of line.

The small muscles of the hand get a workout in these games, along with the awareness of how to assess their energy output to produce the desired results.

Games for Social Skills

We humans are social animals. Like it or not, we are born with a need to be part of a community. Some of us don't like it.

Children with difficulties in social skills may demonstrate a preference for solitary play, have difficultly forming friendships, and be slower to develop play skills than their peers.

Social participation is a complex process in which we are required to share attention, understand social cues, problem-solve, and regulate our own responses.

Being social can be a real problem area for kids who have sensory-processing problems. Social skills are all mixed in with the sensory pathways. Children may be uncomfortable in a social setting because the noise level is too high and their auditory pathway is overstimulated. Maybe there is something odd about the smell of another. Or the food at the social gathering is fine for others, but distasteful to them.

But we can help. Our detective skills and our children's increasing ability to articulate their discomfort can help us figure out where the problem lies and respect their sensory idiosyn-crasies—and when possible, work around them.

GOALS OF THE GAMES

The first step toward social awareness is shared attention. Shared attention is when two people are noticing the same thing at the same time. If you say, "Hey, look at that red bird," and your child looks up to see the bird, that's shared attention. But some children won't look up to see the bird; in fact, they may not even act as if they heard you, or if they did, they don't care about that bird, or any bird.

So, if we want to create a shared-attention moment, we should figure out what interests the child. It might be trains or dinosaurs or food. We can then help them explore the interest, and incorporate others in that interest so it becomes part of their social repertoire—something they can do happily with others.

Sharing attention with your child, whether you're both noticing a cloud that looks like a bunny or playing Candy Land, gives your child a self-esteem boost.

The social games in this chapter use play as the medium, which encourages children to engage with others in shared-attention moments. The games I chose minimize the sensory aspect and maximize the pleasure of doing things with others. It may be as simple as stacking cans to make a tower together or as complex as inventing a dance. The goal is to find playful ways that children can feel part of the group.

People Glue | 2 YEARS TO 7 YEARS

You've probably been in a social situation when you didn't know what to say. You felt awkward. Life for a child with sensory differences is hard enough, so in a potentially awkward time, it's helpful to stick with a child's strengths.

This game is for the child who likes to feel squeezed and deeply touched. This game is for the kid who loves the Hot Dog with Cushions and Mustard game as described in chapter 9, the chapter on movement.

You pretend you have a jar of magic glue. You might demonstrate by "gluing" your hands together, then trying with all your might to take them apart. You can't. You can't until you blow on them with your—of course—magic breath!

Now you glue your child and a friend together. Pretend to put glue down the sides of each of them, and then glue their sides together so that they are both facing front. Have them put their arms around each other, too. Glue their other arms down, too, if need be.

Challenge the glued duo to jump to a specified place together. The game can be short and they must go from a chair to the sofa. Or it could be long and they go the whole length of the yard.

If you want to get the sillies out, glue different parts of them together. How far can they go with their foreheads glued?

Masses of Bubbles | 2 YEARS TO 12 YEARS

 You need a big bowl, like a large salad bowl, along with water, liquid dishwashing soap, and one straw per person. Squirt about one tablespoon of liquid dish soap into a bowl, and fill the bowl one-third full of water.

The game is to blow through the straw into the bowl, but the delight is watching the bubble monster grow and grow. With everyone all blowing together, see how big it can become before it topples spectacularly over the rim of the bowl.

Many children like to then pop the bubbles with their fingers. If you're worried that your child will suck up the bubbles rather than blow them, you can make a little cut near the top of the straw that will prevent liquid from going into their mouth.

You can vary the challenge with the size of the straw. Aquarium tubing works well, and you can cut to the length you wish. The longer or wider the straw, the more muscle control you need to blow.

A Kid Sandwich | 3 YEARS TO 7 YEARS

Have the children stand in a circle. Pick one child to stand in the center of the circle and be the bread. Then ask, "What else shall we put in this sandwich?" If the children don't come up with ideas right away, suggest some. Say, "Let's add some cheese," and then pick another child to be the cheese! Place the "cheese" on the "bread," and continue with ingredients such as ham, pickles, tomato, lettuce, and so on, and end with another piece of "bread." Each time, place the child in front of the last ingredient. You can be the one who picks the child who will be each ingredient, but you'll probably find, as I do, that they are jumping up and down excitedly to be the next piece. You might also find that some children might call out an ingredient that isn't usually in a sandwich, such as rice or chocolate. Go ahead and put whatever they say in the sandwich!

After the sandwich is made, squeeze all the ingredients together by putting your arms around all the children and squeezing them together. Announce, "It's time to eat," and everyone that is not part of the sandwich can pretend to eat, smacking their lips and making chewing sounds. Yum!

Then start all over and make a new sandwich!

This is a wonderful game to play with children who have sensory differences, because they might have difficulty being social the conventional way, but being squeezed next to another is a whole other story. It provides the proprioceptive feedback that children with SPD often crave, as well as the friendliness, warmth, and inclusion of connecting with another human in a nonthreatening and silly way.

Children are also experimenting here with playing pretend. They are pretending to be part of a sandwich, and everyone pretending together reinforces their sense of being part of the group. Some children might prefer watching for a few turns before being part of the game. That's fine, too. They can be part of the eating crew and pretend to eat the delicious sandwich!

Hidden Message | 3 YEARS TO 7 YEARS

 Watching something appear from nothing feeds a child's delight in magic. In this game, each player writes a letter or draws on a white piece of paper or index card with a white wax candle or a white crayon. Since the shape or drawing is made with something white, it can't be seen well until it's painted.

The game is to hand out index cards (they are better than paper because they are a little heavier) to each player. Have everyone draw whatever they want. Shapes like circles and triangles are good to start with since they are easiest to do.

After everyone is done, they hand another person their card. Then that person, using paint and a paintbrush, paint over the wax shape. The magic part happens now, because when the children paint over the paper, the shape or drawing suddenly appears!

Bingo markers with a sponge top are also good to use to paint over the wax. Bingo markers spread out the paint and don't need as much control as a paintbrush.

Can You Do What I Do?
Can You Say What I Say? | 3 YEARS TO 10 YEARS

With those two simple lines, you can open up a social world of imitation and being in sync with others. In this game, the chant "Can you do what I do? Can you say what I say?" is repeated, and the first person does whatever sound and hand or finger motion she wants. The other players all imitate that sound and the accompanying gesture. Then the next person has a turn, and everyone imitates that movement and sound.

The beauty of the game is that there are no wrong sounds and no wrong movements. A hand movement without a sound is okay, and vice versa. The game is just for the fun of creating and imitating with others. It also reinforces taking turns, another important social skill.

If a child decides that standing and jumping is the movement they want to do, then everyone stands and jumps.

Children who are nonverbal can join in because the game only requires gestures and sounds, not words. For kids who are uncomfortable with attention, gestures are short, so there is just a burst of attention that passes by quickly.

A simple example of movement with sound might be 10 fingers wagging and the sound be "La-la-la-la-la-lu." It may not look funny on paper, but everybody wagging and "la-la-lu-ing" together is silly fun that, most importantly, kids are doing in sync with one another.

Art Day | 3 YEARS TO 12 YEARS

Creating art with others can be a stress-free way to be together if the medium is simple to use and the results unique. In this art, everyone, regardless of skill or previous experience, can join in to create equally grand artist pieces.

To accomplish this, start by giving all the children eyedroppers or medicine droppers. If they have never used an eyedropper before, start the game by showing them how to fill an eyedropper with water and how to release the water.

Once they have the idea, change the water to water-based paint. Have the children fill up their eyedroppers with paint or water dyed with food coloring.

Lay out a big piece of paper. Children each take a turn to drop some paint from their eyedropper. Hold the dropper low, just above the paper. On each successive turn, everyone gets to drop the paint from their eyedropper at higher and higher distances. Notice the difference in the results, depending on how far the paint drops.

Once there is plenty of paint on the paper, the children can stand around the painting and blow on the puddles and change the look of the work. They could also use straws and blow the paint around, or take turns tilting the paper one way and another to change the painting.

Other possibilities are to press another sheet of white paper on top to get a duplicate design, or fold the painted paper in half and get a whole new design.

You might want to play around with different things to paint on. Instead of using dry paper, wet it first. You could use wax paper, cardboard, or aluminum foil instead of regular paper or use burlap, wood, grocery bags, or rocks for different results. If eyedropper art loses its novelty, there is no end of other possible things to paint with. Try sponges, cotton balls, powder puffs, toothbrushes, shoe brushes, cotton swabs, and corks.

The best part of this kind of artwork is that everything looks good. Jackson Pollock and his ilk of painters made a whole new form of art famous by splattering paint this way and that.

You might want to take a group photo with all the variations these proud children did together on their art day.

Crazy Handshakes and Nutty Dances | 3 YEARS TO 12 YEARS

 In the olden days, about 20 years ago, a handshake was a simple, regular thing. You reached out with your right hand, connected with the other person's right hand, and shook up and down.

Today, anything goes. The beauty of that is children are free to make up their own handshake, and they can have a different handshake with different people. You and your child can have a secret one, or one that you can teach others. If you have a small social group, say, just the family or dearest friends or close neighborhood kids, you can practice it together. And if they want to add sounds or body movement, all the better.

The social skill is about finding the pleasure in relating to others and feeling in sync with them.

If a child has difficulty with too much touch, movements can be geared toward minimal touch, as in handshakes that are done by flipping hands and shaking fingers at each other.

NUTTY DANCE

Like handshakes, dance movements can be made up. A while back, there was something called the Harlem Shake, which was really just people shaking their bodies in no particular pattern or style.

In the Nutty Dance, players stand in a circle and make up a

dance, movement by movement. The first person does a movement, any movement—swaying side to side or a twirl or a straight leg kick, anything they want. Everyone copies that move.

The next player adds a new movement, and—here is the crucial part—everyone *first* does the first person's movement and *then* adds the second movement to that.

When the third person does their own unique movement, everyone must do the first movement, then the second, then the third.

See how it goes? It becomes a dance with separate movements that are all the movements put together in the order they were created. Each person can also add a silly sound to their movement if they want.

The Nutty Dance is as much about remembering all the moves as it is about doing the moves. But, in truth, it only takes one or two people to have good memory retention. The others can just follow, if need be. The best part is that everyone dances together.

Since all the movements are short, children who have difficulty with imitating body moves will be able to do these quick and simple moves and still feel like part of the gang.

Can You Can Can | 3 YEARS TO 12 YEARS

 If you have a slew of aluminum cans, you can set up a game that takes focusing and muscle control—oh yes, and is fun to play with others. It does take a little time to gather and wash out the cans, but if my experience is any guide, it will be worth it. Kids want to play with cans. Along with string and boxes, cans are valuable toys.

Put all the cans in a laundry basket. Ten is a good amount. Have the child sit on the floor facing you.

You want to control this game in the beginning by keeping the basketful of cans with you. Later, your child can get free rein to play with them.

Put down one can, and then demonstrate putting another can carefully on top of that. Next, you hand your child a can to put directly on top of yours. Keep stacking, turn by turn, until all the cans fall over with a wonderful clatter.

Stacking the cans precisely makes the tower taller and rewards your child for using good motor control.

Gather them back up into the laundry basket and start again.

I like to sing a song while playing this game so I can alter the speed from slow motion to fast as you can:

Can can,
Can you do the can can?
Can you do the can can?
Can can can can.

If you've never heard of that song, don't worry. I made up this version. Any song or lyrics will do if you want to set the rhythm. I might start by singing a song very slowly until the child is successful, and then speeding it up a bit. Ridiculously fast is very okay, too.

Be My Mirror | 3 YEARS TO 12 YEARS

 Start this game off with a question: "Can you do this with your face?" Then wink one eye, then the other. Can your child wink either eye?

Keep adding possibilities and changing the challenge:

- Cross your eyes.
- Touch your tongue to your nose.
- Raise one eyebrow.
- Raise the other one.
- Wiggle your ears.
- Curl your tongue.
- Do "raspberries" with your lips.

It's best to take turns playing this game, because you might be surprised at the facial tricks your child can do that you can't.

If you want new possibilities, present different emotions to change your facial features:

- What does a sad face look like?
- What about tragic or pathetic?
- Show happy, then elated.
- Let mad turn into furious.
- Does frustrated look different than confused?

There is no end to this game, because you could also act out a type of person. You can try out dramatic or silly or scary poses. Here are a few examples:

- haughty queen
- happy tourist
- mean monster
- confused student
- silly clown
- rock and roll superstar

You can use just your faces if you're sitting down, which makes it a good game to play when waiting for food at a restaurant, or anytime you are stuck waiting somewhere and want to keep your child engaged.

When you're home, you can play this same game using your whole body. You and your child stand and face each other. Take turns pretending that one of you is the mirror and one is the person looking into the mirror. That person who is looking into the mirror moves very slowly, as if doing a slow-motion dance, and the other has to imitate or mirror their exact movements. You can start slow and gradually vary the speed.

You are giving your child the social experience of being in tune with one another, but this game also uses the movement sense. Children learn skills by watching others do them, so being able to imitate someone's movement is an important skill for learning and a useful sense to strengthen.

Dialing the Stations | 5 YEARS TO 12 YEARS

We want the child who finds some noises intolerable to find strategies that will allow control over the amount of auditory input dealt with. In this radio game, the child can play around with the level of sound to a tolerable place, and have a bit of fun with you and any family members or friends in the car or at home.

In the game, you use a radio that is unplugged, or use the car radio when the motor is off. Your child gets to be the radio stations, and you get to be the dialer—or vice versa. The dialer hits a button or turns the dial, and the other sings a song or makes up a fake newscast, gives a weather report, or hosts a talk show. The dialer has the option of making the sound louder or softer, as well as changing the dial. This is an important detail, because you are also looking to find the volume levels that are tolerable. If your child usually complains that your beautiful singing voice is uncomfortable to listen to, here is an opportunity to find out if your child is okay with your softer sound.

This game can be a lot of creative fun for you and your child. If your child loves to imitate people on TV or radio, here is an opportunity to show off those skills. It's empowering for both of you, in a giggling sort of way, to switch stations right in the middle of the other's "broadcast." And the information you both get on what's an acceptable volume is helpful when working out life strategies. Your child might find, for example, that loud talking is painful, but that talking that's muted with earplugs makes things just right. You might even find that the novelty of the game can increase tolerance just by having fun with possibilities.

Appendices

Appropriate Toys | APPENDIX A

If you think children with sensory differences require toys that aren't available at a regular toy store, think again. You just have to know which ones would be especially helpful. For example, nothing beats an old-fashioned pogo stick to teach children balance right along with new no-pedal balance bikes.

Scratch-and-sniff markers sharpen smell and learning the fingering techniques on a ukelele teaches dexterity. Refer to the list below to get the sense of which kind of toys are helpful and visit each website for more.

WEBSITES

autism-products.com/Autism_Toys_s/54.htm

fatbraintoys.com/special_needs/sensory_integration_disorder.cfm

mamaot.com/ultimate-gift-list-for-sensory-seekers

sensorysmarts.com/toys_and_equipment.html

therapyshoppe.com/category/1423-sensory-integration

TYPES OF TOYS

GROSS MOTOR

- swing
- hammock
- inflatable cushion
- trampoline
- rocking board
- Sit 'n Spin
- pogo stick
- parachute
- stepping cans
- tunnels
- tents

- balls
- Velcro catchers
- darts
- scooter
- balance beam
- T-stools
- Bilibo
- horse rider
- balancing board

- bungee jumper
- teeter-totter
- hopscotch mat
- Twister
- balance bike
- gymnastic ball
- scooter board
- skateboard
- jump rope
- scarves

FINE MOTOR

- snap beads
- crayons and paper
- putty
- play dough
- Etch-A-Sketch
- Mr. Potato Head
- lacing toys
- puzzles
- child-size scissors
- beads and string
- dot-to-dot number game
- mazes
- nesting cups
- tracing paper
- Candy Land
- punch-ball balloon
- coloring books
- stickers
- drawing cartoon book
- pretend sand
- fake snow
- oil-based clay
- air-dry clay
- ukulele
- guitar
- origami
- puppets
- markers
- tweezers and tongs
- eyedroppers
- chopsticks
- pencil grips
- Connect Four
- checkers
- chess
- punching bag
- magnets
- parquetry
- dominoes
- blocks
- Wikki Stix
- piano or keyboard

SENSORY

- earmuffs
- polarized sunglasses
- earplugs
- sleep mask
- weighted blanket or vest
- vibrating toys and pillow
- nature-sound CD
- essential oil
- timer/stopwatch
- chewable jewelry
- chewable pencil topper
- water table
- sensory brush
- Koosh ball
- seamless socks
- whistles
- squeezable balls
- textured beanbags
- musical instruments
- beanbag chair
- bingo
- tents
- listening lotto game
- seated cushions
- whisper phone
- light filters
- vibrating toothbrush
- Lava Lamp
- scented play dough
- scented markers
- scratch-and-sniff stickers
- I Spy books or cards
- Mad Libs books

Heavy Work List | APPENDIX B

Consider how you feel after engaging in physical activity. Likely, you're more centered, more present, and much calmer. When children work their major muscle groups, it can have this same effect—especially with SPD kids. There are opportunities to engage your child in this kind of sensory stimulation, or heavy work, everywhere. I've included some options below, but I encourage you to make them your own and come up with others—think about activities requiring strength or movement, and you've got the right idea.

AT HOME

- Carry in the groceries.
- Paint the outside walls of the house with water.
- Get the wet clothes out of the washer and into the dryer.
- Pull a wagon with weeds in it.
- Dig a hole for a plant.
- Hoe the weeds in the garden.
- Sweep the kitchen floor.
- Wash windows.
- Ride a skateboard.
- Take out the trash.
- Carry books from one place to another.
- Move the furniture to set up an obstacle course.
- Wash the car.
- Rake leaves.
- Shovel snow.
- Build a snowman.
- Have pillow fights.
- Do a zillion push-ups and sit-ups.
- Carry full laundry baskets, and deliver the clean clothes.

OUTDOORS

- Hike on a trail.
- Push a toddler in a stroller.
- Play tag.
- Do races in the playground.
- Walk the neighborhood.
- Practice gymnastics.
- Wrestle.
- Go swimming.
- Run or walk in sand.
- Learn karate.
- Try tai chi.
- Jump on trampoline.
- Run in a race.
- Race on a dirt bike.
- Skateboard in the park.
- Play neighborhood basketball.
- Go horseback riding.

AT SCHOOL

- Jump rope.
- Play hopscotch.
- Catch and throw balls.
- Carry books in library.
- Stack chairs.
- Play in sandbox.
- Do sit-ups.
- Run races.
- Wash windows.
- Chalk sidewalks.
- Climb on jungle gym.
- Dance in gym.
- Play foursquare.
- Swing at recess.

All children need at least 60 minutes of exercise per day, but some aren't excited by that prospect and prefer TV, computer, phone, or tablet screens over breaking a sweat. I recommend making a contract with your child: Doing heavy work earns equivalent screen time. I've listed some examples here but encourage you to develop whatever works for your child.

- **Swim for 40 minutes.** Get to use computer for 40 minutes.

- **Take wet laundry out of the washer and put it in the dryer.** Get 20 minutes of hassle-free screen time.

- **Ride bike in neighborhood for 20 minutes.** Get 20 minutes of screen time.

- **Do whatever chores are needed.** Get equivalent screen time in return.

You and your child can negotiate the terms of the contract. It can be the same heavy work every day or vary throughout the week. Choices can depend on preferences, but make the contract nonnegotiable once it's agreed upon. Use the "first this, then that" rule: first work, then computer.

Success Stories and Life Lessons | APPENDIX C

I've had the opportunity to work around the world with children from all walks of life. Over the years, my work has brought me a great sense of joy and satisfaction. Children have learned and progressed and blossomed right before my eyes, and sometimes I am the one who learns—from them.

What I've learned is to be human and to know and appreciate all the aspects of being a human being—our strengths, our weaknesses, our uniqueness.

The stories are countless, and many will resonate with me always. I share some in hopes that you will relate to the profound moments that can bloom from thoughtful time spent in the moment, paying attention to a child.

GAINING UNDERSTANDING OF A CONCRETE THINKER

We were in a regular Head Start classroom. Cherry Mae was our special-ed child with Autism Spectrum Disorder (ASD), and we chose a group game that we knew she could play: Throw the Balls into the Box. In this game, the children throw balls made out of newspaper into an opened box. Unbeknownst to the children, the flaps on the bottom of the box have also been opened, but are loosely closed so I can lift up the box and all the balls fall out the bottom.

The game, besides encouraging eye-hand coordination, is mainly intended to teach the prepositions, such as in front, behind, beside, and inside. First we sing a song about throwing the balls into the box, and the children throw their handmade newspaper balls into the box. Then I ask the children, "Where are the balls? Are they in front of the box?" and I exaggeratedly look in front. The kids say no. "Are they beside the box?" I do the same mime on either side, and the kids respond again, no. "Are they behind?" No again, shouted this time. "Are they inside?" At this point I pick up the box and shake it slightly, and all the balls come flooding out. The kids get all excited and want to play again immediately. Again, once the box is full, I pretend to be looking for the balls, and the kids happily respond.

Not Cherry Mae. Though she was delighted the first time, she looked at me questioningly the second time. By the third, her patience had worn thin. Cherry Mae is intelligent and loves academics, but she is a very concrete thinker, which leaves little room for playful imagination. She came up to me and gave me a serious lecture. Some of it was in her own Cherry Mae babble, but the meaning was clear: "What are you, an idiot? The balls are in the box. Why do you keep asking? Can't you see?"

Before she lost all respect for my intelligence, we had to stop playing the game that I had planned specifically for Cherry Mae. We ended up throwing the lightweight newspaper balls at different targets such as "something red" or "something square" to coincide with her academic interests and still include my eye-hand coordination goal!

And now, when I plan an activity, I keep concrete thinkers in mind, with a smile.

EVERYBODY'S GOT THEIR SOMETHING

Nikolai walked into the room screaming. His mother had told him he was going to stay with his teachers in the game room, but she wasn't staying with him. He had always been with either his mom or his nanny, and even one moment without them was too long. "He shower with me. He sleep with me. It too much," his Russian mom complained. Mom left, and a teacher tried to console him. Nikolai didn't notice. He ran to the window sobbing; he had never been on his own, and for all he knew, he would not be okay. I suggested to the teacher that Nikolai sit on his lap to just watch what the others were doing.

The others were taking turns on a seesaw that was improvised out of a two-by-six and a rocker board. The kids took turns sitting on either end of the board and going up and down. A third child was in the center of the board, and they all giggled from the fun sensations.

Their joyous sounds finally captured Nikolai's attention. He watched and got quieter. When the game was over, the kids were given plastic garbage bags to put over their clothes so they could paint. When Nikolai reached for a garbage bag and said "Plastic," we knew we had him.

He joined the others who were dipping pieces of banana stalk, cut from the stem of the plant, into paints and pressing the stalks onto poster paper that had been placed on the wall. We used potato pieces and celery stalks as well as small brushes that fit on their fingers. Shallow bowls of red, blue, and yellow paints were placed on the covered floor.

The children were entranced, especially Nikolai. Even another child who had been diagnosed with ADHD had no trouble staying with the activity for the entire period.

To capture a child's attention, it's important to know what interests him. Some people like to do puzzles. Some people love to play in water. Some only respond strongly to movement. Nikolai, we know now, is an "art" person. We'll be ready to entice him again with art so he can continue to experience that life, even without Mommy present, can still be good.

Adapted from Barbara Sher, "Nikolai Finds Art," The Whole Spectrum of Social, Motor, and Sensory Games (San Francisco: Jossey-Bass, 2013).

EMBRACING NOVELTY

We know that children pay attention when something is novel. We also know that children on the spectrum sometimes have difficulty with change. Sitting with seven preschool children who were diagnosed with autism or SPD, I wanted to play novel games that gave kids the opportunity to experience changes.

This could be challenging, I thought.

I was having them take turns digging into a box of sand and pulling out one of the buried plastic animals. They kept passing the sandbox to the next person. The game was going well, but by the fourth turn, I could sense they were fading.

"Pick up the sand, and make a waterfall," I improvised, as I lifted up a handful of sand and let it trickle out of my hand, in the lovely way sand does. The kids perked up and excitedly imitated me when it was their turn with the sandbox. I sang a simple song so they would learn that their turn lasted as long as the song, and then it was the next person's turn.

They all had had a bunch of turns when the novelty began to wear off. I changed the game again and sang a new song (sung to the tune of "London Bridge Is Falling Down"):

Make a circle in the sand, in the sand, in the sand.
Make a circle in the sand.
Look how [child's name] can!

Everyone now wanted a turn to stick their finger deep into the sand, make a circle, and hear their name praised.

The tasks kept changing. Sometimes the game was about transferring sand back and forth from one hand to another; sometimes it was about putting sandpiles on the table and writing letters in them.

The last game was pouring water in the sand and poking holes; it came with another song (sung to the tune of "Row, Row, Row Your Boat"):

Poke, poke, poke a hole; poke it all you can.
Poke and poke and poke and poke.
Right into the sand.

The kids loved all the games, but I knew they were also learning social awareness, bilateral movement, letter recognition, attention focusing, turn taking, finger isolation, tactile sensations, and the acceptance of changes.

But the kids might have missed those nuances; for them, it was just plain fun.

WORKING THROUGH FEAR

Leandro was diagnosed with autism. To his mom, dad, and even me—his therapist—a better description would be "difficult." Very difficult. Leandro had opinions, and mostly they were "No." He would only eat certain things; he wouldn't do this, and he didn't like that. Mostly his folks dealt with him by letting him do what he wanted. He was intelligent and obstinate.

When I first came to his house for a home visit, he refused to do any of the activities I had brought in my bag. Finally I brought out the sure-to-engage-children-on-the spectrum toy: something with lights and sounds and movement. He grabbed that and played with it exclusively, not even letting his sister have a look. When it was time for me to go, he had a royal meltdown.

On succeeding visits, he became more interested in my other activities. He used the word "share," which meant that you share with him, not that he would share with you. He approached his life with a rigid attitude that things had to go his way, or else.

His parents were understandably relieved when it was time for him to go to preschool at the local Head Start program. His teachers became less enthusiastic. Leandro would not follow the rules. He wouldn't eat at mealtime, he wouldn't sit in a circle, he wouldn't play with others, and he didn't like to be touched.

The only thing he would respond to was a firm voice. He was learning the rule: First you do this; then you can do that. He didn't like the rule.

I brought in a group movement activity so he could learn how to play with others. The first time, I brought in a simple London

Bridge game, where kids went under a bridge made of foam pool noodles, and at a certain moment in the songs, the kids under the bridge would get caught between the noodles. The kids laughed and couldn't wait to get "caught." Leandro's whole body was moving and excited in his space, but he refused to join in. Uncharacteristically, he stayed near the action instead of the other side of the room.

The next time I brought in hula-hoops and laid them on the floor, and the game was to jump from hoop to hoop. I knew that Leandro loved to jump, and sure enough, with just some encouragement, he was jumping from hoop to hoop. Each time I rewarded him with a big smile and a high five.

Next, I changed the game, which I always do to add variation, and made the hoops into a tunnel that children would crawl through. I sang a song about tunnels, and the kids excitedly crawled through. Except Leandro. He refused. His aide practically pushed him through the first hoop while Leandro voiced his reluctance, but he went through the rest by himself, and by the second go-through, he went by himself. Afterward, with a big proud smile, he came over to me for a high five / fist bump. I was delighted and surprised to see how proud he was of such an easy activity.

And then I changed the game again. To reward him, I put the hoop back to lying flat on the floor but in a zigzag pattern so players would jump again. Sideways this time. All the kids played the new game.

Except Leandro. He completely and utterly refused. I encouraged. He wouldn't budge. I let it go, as it was time to end the game anyway.

And then as I was writing up my notes, I got it about him. He was afraid of new things. He was *afraid* of changes. He felt safer sticking to what he knew. No wonder he was reluctant. He wasn't sure he *could* do it the new way.

When the other children were elsewhere, I sat quietly beside him, and for his ears only I talked about how much he had learned since he was a baby. It was scary to learn new things, but he had done it, and now he could walk and run and jump and hop and draw and write. The whole time Leandro sat still and attentive. Then his posture changed, and he leaned against me and quietly put his hand on my arm. "You're a terrific kid," I said, realizing later he probably didn't hear that much.

The teacher had put out little cups of squash for the children to taste. I took one cup and ate one and offered the other to him, a very reluctant eater. He first tightened his lips and then softly opened his mouth to taste one. I popped one in. He chewed it up. I offered him another. He reached in the cup to pick it up, but it was too mushy for him to touch, so I got it for him. He ate it, and then we went to the table for lunch, and he ate a whole hamburger bun with lots of ketchup (hold the meat).

I asked for a kiss when it was time to go, and he kissed me softly on the cheek.

I had made a friend, and I learned, again, to recognize and respect the fear that's under the refusal.

HAVING FUN AROUND THE HOUSE

I want to be more like Mary Poppins. Instead of screeching at my children, like the Wicked Witch of the West, to clean up yet another big mess they've made, I want to burst into song and, with that "spoonful of sugar," watch the work get done. I want to be Poppins-esque not only because it would make me feel better about my mothering, but also because I know how important play is. Over the years, I have devised some games that I use with my own and other children to make the things we have to do more enjoyable. I don't use games every time, but whenever I do, a potentially bad moment is turned into a fun one.

Play, humor, and laughter release a hormonal natural high. It's organic, it's free, and it's an all-natural joy jumper—and best of all, it gets the job done.

Pile It Up

I came up with this lighthearted way of clearing up a mess when I'd returned from an out-of-town workshop, and my young daughters had been left in the company of their loving but not particularly tidy father. I came home to two very happy, healthy girls, but to get to them I had to wade through five days of strewn clothes, game pieces, stale slices of toast, and other flotsam and jetsam. I was delighted to be home, and, fresh from a workshop on singing games for children, I wanted to keep my good mood, practice what I'd learned—and get this overwhelming cleaning job done.

I decided to throw everything, regardless of what it was, into one big pile in the middle of the room, then sort it all out. To the tune of "The Bear Went Over the Mountain," I began tossing everything into the pile while singing, "Put everything in a pi-ile, put everything in a pi-ile, put everything in a pi-*IIIILE*—in the middle of the room! The middle of the room, the middle of the room, put everything in a pi-*IIIILE*—in the middle of the room!"

My five-year-old was immediately suspicious that this might be work, but I reminded her that it had to get done no matter what, so we might as well have some fun. She understood, and she and her sister and I tossed everything that was out of place onto the pile, singing and giggling as we made long shots and high tosses.

The rooms were quickly cleared of debris, except for the big mound in the middle of the living room. We sat around it as if at a campfire. I held up each item and, in rhythmic singsong, said, "A sock, a sock, where does it go?" Someone would answer "The laundry basket!" We did this for each item, and soon the big pile had been separated into smaller piles of books, blankets, laundry, toys, and so on. Everyone was then assigned some piles to put away while I swept the floor. Within a relatively short time, the house was inhabitable again, and we were all still in good moods.

Pile It on the Bed, Too

We've since used this method often, whenever my daughters' bedrooms—or mine—get in that state of overwhelming messiness. At these times we pile everything on the bed so that the floor and all other areas are clear. Once that's done, the project feels doable— now only one pile on the bed needs sorting, instead of the entire room. You can organize the "putting away" aspect according to your child's skill level. A mobile child who can sort will be able to put objects in the correct drawer or shelf. Another child might need to have the toy basket put near her chair, and her job is to toss the toys in the basket. Another child might do best at just dropping dirty clothes in the hamper.

I don't have a song for this work, but having an uncluttered house again and everyone helping in their way sure makes me feel like singing.

Adapted from Barbara Sher, " What Would Mary Poppins Do?," *Parenting Special Needs Magazine*, May–June 2011

THE MAGIC OF SONG

When my children were young, we took a trip to Mexico in a VW bus, with a rowboat my husband made tied to the top. To entertain ourselves on the long ride, we sang every song we knew and learned others from each other. We developed quite a repertoire and used it many times in the years ahead. We even had a couple we thought of as our "family songs."

Singing together always cheered us.

On the most difficult day of our lives, the day we went to the mortuary to say our final good-byes to that wonderful, rowboat-making father, we felt at a loss for words. Then spontaneously we began to sing our songs. The family songs. The silly songs. Even in the midst of that painful moment, singing made us smile and taught me about the enchanted power of song.

Years later, my oldest sent me a CD of our songs. She had gone on the Internet and found versions of each one. They were all there, all our family songs: "Zip-a-Dee-Doo-Dah," "Lollipop, Lollipop," "Side by Side," "Catch a Falling Star," and many others. I was delighted and astounded that she remembered them all.

Maybe inspired by that or just my own propensity for singing, I taught her children, my grandchildren, the family songs. When we would go for hikes in the woods or were searching for salamanders along the creek, I would sing these songs. I was pleased how quickly the boys would memorize some lyrics.

One day in their car, their mom played the CD of our family songs. My grandkids, ages five and seven, thought the music was playing on the radio and innocently figured that station must be called the "Bubbie" station and everyone—everywhere—sang our songs.

Adapted from Barbara Sher, "Rise Up Singing," *Spirit Games: 300 Fun Activities That Bring Children Comfort and Joy* (San Francisco: Jossey-Bass, 2002).

Index